The Long Game on the Silk Road

US and EU Strategy for Central Asia and the Caucasus

S. Frederick Starr
Svante E. Cornell

ROWMAN & LITTLEFIELD
Lanham • Boulder • New York • London

Published in association with the American Foreign Policy Council

Published by Rowman & Littlefield
A wholly owned subsidiary of The Rowman & Littlefield Publishing Group, Inc.
4501 Forbes Boulevard, Suite 200, Lanham, Maryland 20706
www.rowman.com

Unit A, Whitacre Mews, 26-34 Stannary Street, London SE11 4AB

British Library Cataloguing in Publication Information Available

Library of Congress Cataloging-in-Publication Data

Library of Congress Control Number: 2018931212

ISBN 978-1-5381-1463-6 (cloth: alk. paper)
ISBN 978-1-5381-1464-3 (paper: alk. paper)
ISBN 978-1-5381-1465-0 (electronic)

♾™ The paper used in this publication meets the minimum requirements of American National Standard for Information Sciences—Permanence of Paper for Printed Library Materials, ANSI/NISO Z39.48-1992.

Printed in the United States of America

CONTENTS

Acknowledgements 4

1. Introduction 5

2. Setting the Scene: Central Asia and the Caucasus, 1991-2016 15

3. Western Activity and Achievements in the Caucasus and Central Asia ...39

4. A Deeper Look: Shortcomings of Western Policy 75

5. Structural Problems and their Solutions 108

6. Updating and Upgrading Strategic Assumptions and Practices 121

7. The Way Ahead .... .151

Authors .... .157

Index .... .158

ACKNOWLEDGEMENTS

The authors would like to express their gratitude to staff members and interns with the American Foreign Policy Council and Institute for Security and Development Policy who helped make this book possible. Đorđe Milošević provided valuable research assistance, as did Jack Verser. Frank Esparraga and Alec Forss assisted with editing and layout. Beyond that, the authors are indebted to dozens of officials, diplomats, bureaucrats and scholars from the United States, Europe, and the region itself with whom they have interacted over the past two decades, and whose insights have helped form the arguments made in this book. Needless to say, those arguments, and any errors, are those of the authors themselves

INTRODUCTION

The beginning of 2017 marked a momentous anniversary for countries that were once part of the Soviet Union. A quarter century had now passed since the Communist behemoth unexpectedly collapsed, giving rise to independent statehood that some nations actively welcomed but others viewed with trepidation. This twenty-fifth anniversary invites assessments of progress since independence of all the newly formed states. Indeed, such retrospection is taking place everywhere from Tallinn to Tashkent. But it is also an occasion to evaluate the nature and effectiveness of American and European policies toward those states. There is no question that western leaders at the time fully understood the magnitude of the developments taking place before their eye, and that these momentous changes demanded from them far-reaching and wise strategies. Twenty-five years later it is fair to evaluate the results of the policies they adopted and also to take a fresh look at the assumptions on which they were based. Have the policies in place served American and European interests? Where they have not, how can they be improved? And above all, after a quarter century have these countries become more relevant to western interests, or less so?

These are the questions this book will address, focusing on the South Caucasus and Central Asia, or the so-called "southern" region of the former Soviet Union. From west to east, this includes Georgia, Armenia, Azerbaijan, Kazakhstan, Turkmenistan, Uzbekistan, Kyrgyzstan and Tajikistan.

This introduction lays out the case for this book. It argues that these countries, because of their intrinsic characteristics and of developments in the regions surrounding them, matter more to America and Europe today than they did twenty-five years ago. While these states differ greatly from one another, their commonalities and interdependencies are sufficient for America and Europe to treat them regionally, as well as bilaterally. And while western policies toward these countries have given rise to impressive achievements, structural and conceptual mistakes have hampered and diminished them. These flaws have caused the West to mishandle some opportunities and to miss others. As a result, the West has yet to realize the full potential of positive relations between the West and countries of the region. For this to happen, western analysts and policymakers must fully grasp what actually happened during the first twenty-five years of relations. But the significance of the past quarter-century of these relations extends beyond the region itself. Indeed, they present in microcosm a case study of American and European foreign policy as a whole during the post-Cold War era.

IS THERE A REGION?

A skeptical reader may well ask whether such disparate states should all be treated in the same volume. After all, the main and most immediate link between them is their common Soviet past and their differences. These were already significant at the time of independence and have only grown since independence. What do Armenia and Tajikistan have in common today? Should mental habits formed in Soviet times not be discarded in favor of novel new ways of viewing the world? And even if the South Caucasus and Central Asia constitute distinctive regions, are the differences between them not so great as to demand separate treatment in a study of this sort?

We would be the first to argue that viewing these states solely in a post-Soviet context would be an extreme form of reductionism. It is a fact that ancient links severed by Soviet boundaries are re-emerging and that some old habits and values are reappearing. The various countries of Central Asia and the Caucasus are rediscovering traditional relations with Europe, the Middle East, and South and East Asia. Indeed, parts of Turkey and Iran are intricately linked with the Caucasus, leading two local scholars to advance the notion that what we call the South Caucasus is really the "Central Caucasus", and that adjacent provinces of Turkey and Iran should be called the southwest and southeast Caucasus, respectively.[1] Similarly, Afghanistan and Xinjiang have traditionally been understood to form integral parts of Greater Central Asia, and this is once again gradually becoming reality.[2]

If the past twenty-five years have proven anything, it is that statehood matters. The eight nations under consideration no longer see their destinies determined solely by a single and distant imperial center. They have been able to engage on the world stage both with the East and West and their neighbors in every direction. Because they are all relatively small states encircled by the most powerful states on the Eurasian continent, the task of establishing their sovereignty in actual fact and not just on paper has been particularly challenging. They also face the common challenge of being landlocked, which significantly complicates their interactions with the rest of the world. And they all also face the challenge of overcoming the vestiges of the Soviet system and of its lingering impact on the mentality of citizens of the new states. These facts alone justify our treating the Caucasus and Central Asia, and the two of them together, as in many senses a region. We believe that western foreign policy should do so as well. Further justifying such an approach is the fact that western interests in this part of the world are by their very nature regional and not purely bilateral in character.

Does the Caspian Sea mark a line of division between states to its east and west? In reality, this inland sea unites nations as much as it separates them from one another. Without the Caucasus, Central Asia would be fully encircled by powers many times larger than even the largest regional states; and the Caucasus derives much of its current importance by being the western part of a transport corridor extending across the Caspian into the heart of Asia.

One might also ask why our study does not also include Ukraine, Moldova and Belarus. After all, the European Union's Eastern Partnership program groups countries of the Caucasus with these three states and not with Central Asia. Yet it is important that these countries are squeezed solely between Russia and Europe. While they share many common traits with countries of the Caucasus and Central Asia, their geopolitical environment is fundamentally different from those of Central Asia and the Caucasus, which need to contend with a multitude of influences, not least from the Islamic world, that are not significantly present in the states of Eastern Europe.

However, we firmly acknowledge that Afghanistan is intimately a part of the broader region that is the subject of this book. However, the sheer magnitude and character of western and particularly American involvement in that country over the past fifteen years has been such that it requires a special study.

Do Central Asia and the Caucasus Matter to the West?

Scarcity focuses the mind. Since the financial crisis of 2008, both America and Europe have undergone profound internal convulsions and their governments have suffered deep budget deficits. These have caused western leaders to question the investment of scarce resources and attention in remote areas of the world. True, the United States under President Obama declared a "pivot to Asia" but this did not come to fruition and in any case excluded Central Asia from its definition of "Asia." At the same time he proposed to turn the nation's attention and resources away from troublesome foreign areas in order to focus on "nation-building" at home. Since Brexit, the EU has been under similar pressure. Given this, what is the place of these small countries in the policies of either the EU or U.S.?

This book proceeds from the premise that the importance of the countries of the Caucasus and Central Asia are, to use a tired expression, greater than the sum of their parts. It also will insist that Western engagement there is a matter of leadership and not primarily of financial resources. The war in Georgia in 2008 illustrated this latter point with glaring clarity. The western powers, in the midst of a deep financial crisis, ended up footing the $5 billion bill to deal with the aftermath of the conflict. Had they instead asserted beforehand the kind of political leadership that could have prevented the conflict, the cost would have been far lower.

The importance of the Caucasus and Central Asia lies in their crucial geographical location – as small countries surrounded by the rising powers of the Eurasian continent: Russia, China, India, Pakistan, Iran, and Turkey. With their small populations, they welcome a Western presence because it helps them balance the influence of the behemoths that border them; this makes them , to varying degrees, willing and able partners of the West. Further, their importance derives from their location at the crossing points of both east-west and north-south corridors of transport and trade. For millennia the Caucasus and Central Asia formed the link (or buffer) between Europe and Asia (including both China and India) as well as between northern Europe, Russia, and the Middle East. Thus, the Caucasus and Central Asia should be considered key components of any Western efforts to assure commercial, energy, and security access to the heart of the Eurasian land mass and beyond in every direction.

The importance of the Caucasus and Central Asia can also be stated in terms of the two most salient challenges facing the transatlantic alliance today: Russia's aggressive expansionism, and the Islamic radicalism emanating from the Middle East. These twin challenges are fundamentally reshaping the security environment to Europe's east and south. The Caucasus and Central Asia are sensitive and important pressure points for both issues. The task of countering Putin's new Russian imperialism requires a firm strategy to bolster the states on Russia's southern periphery. At the same time, the Caucasus and Central Asia constitute fully a half of the world's Muslim-majority states that are ruled by secular forms of governments. These states may have far to go in terms of democratic development but, importantly, their governments and populations are committed to the separation of state and religion, to secular laws and courts, and to the protection of their citizens from religious diktats that would curtail basic rights. Thus, the Caucasus and Central Asia are bulwarks both against Moscow and against the Islamic radicalism of the Middle East. Developments within the region further increase the relevance of these nations. China's rise was the leading factor underlying America's "pivot" to Asia. Central Asia, as an area of intensive Chinese economic expansion, must be considered relevant to this concern. In Iran, the theocracy introduced in 1979 seeks to expand its regional influence, as shown by events from Syria to Yemen. In Turkey, the deterioration of secular government has given rise to a growing anti-Western authoritarianism with Islamist underpinnings. And in Afghanistan the US and its western partners spent a trillion dollars and sacrificed several thousand of their young men and women to build a country that hovers today between peace and prosperity or a retreat to a kind of chaos that could once again threaten the West. Together, these diverse developments make the fate of the Caucasus and Central Asia all the more significant a concern for the West.

If the past decade is any guide, we should not be surprised if the areas surrounding the Caucasus and Central Asia – and perhaps the region itself – generate further crises that require a Western response. The spread of disorder in the Levant, a further crisis in Turkey, unrest resulting from the deepening economic crisis in Russia, pauses in China's heretofore unstoppable growth, or the future of nuclear-armed Pakistan – these are only some of the potential developments that might cause the West, in calculating its response, to give serious attention to Central Asia and the Caucasus.

It would be wrong, however, to view the Caucasus and Central Asia solely in terms of possible instability and unrest in their neighborhoods or at home. In fact, the positive prospects for the entire region are even more impressive. Solid growth since independence has put them all within sight of middle class status by mid-century, provided they follow prudent policies. All are seeking to diversify their economies from the limited number of activities developed in Soviet times, and welcome the West's involvement in that process. Moreover, as noted above, geography and politics combine to give these states a central role as transport corridors linking diverse parts of Eurasia. Indeed, these regions are rapidly emerging as a land bridge between the great economies of Europe, China, the Indus region, and the Middle East.

The importance of their role as a transport corridor soared with the expansion of their production of gas and oil and the development of new markets for their energy resources. This has not only provided several of them with an income stream that enables them to consolidate their sovereignty, but it gives western customers and China a direct interest in protecting their production and transport capacities. The creation of the pipeline system connecting the Caspian Sea via Turkey to Europe and also to China enabled Azerbaijan, Kazakhstan, and Turkmenistan to develop their resources free from control by their former colonial overlord. This infrastructure broke the Russian monopoly over the transportation of energy resources. A major portion of Kazakhstan's oil and Turkmenistan's gas resources have yet to come online, so the further potential for the Caucasus and Central Asia to serve as key corridors for these energy resources is considerable.

In the aftermath of the terrorist attacks on New York on September 11, 2001, the U.S. faced the enormous logistic challenge of waging a war in the heart of the Eurasia, thousands of miles from the closest U.S. military bases. The crippling of the Taliban and Al Qaeda in Afghanistan was possible only because the U.S. was able to deliver people and equipment via the Caucasus and Central Asia. When the U.S. expanded its troop levels in Afghanistan a decade later, the Caucasus corridor ensured that NATO forces were not solely dependent upon Pakistan or the Northern Distribution Network (NDN) route across Russia. The importance of this grew clear in early 2014 when, on at least two occasions, Russia prevented the German Air Force from using Russian airspace to supply its military in Afghanistan. The more recent deterioration of U.S.-Russian relations will doubtless cause the Caucasus corridor once more to be a crucial component of any future Western presence in Afghanistan.

Beyond these immediate concerns, the Caucasus and Central Asia are emerging as a major artery of the emerging system of continental trade by land. Most east-west trade between China, India, and Europe at present is conducted by sea and air. But land routes across Eurasia provide a third option that is far cheaper than air travel and much faster than sea routes. This option is fated to become crucial for middle-sized cargo in both directions, and is sure to expand significantly as Indian land routes come open during the coming decade. As in the case of the NDN, the Caucasus-Central Asia corridor is not the only route that exists. But it is the best means of assuring that neither Russia nor Iran has a monopoly over east-west transport. Regional countries themselves have already made significant investments in their port facilities, roads, and railroads. As these new corridors open and as major economies come to depend on them, any eruption of instability or conflict in the Caucasus or Central Asia will pose a threat not just to major Western and regional oil and gas firms, but also to Chinese and Indian producers. However it is viewed, the West has a serious and strategic interest in ensuring the open transport of energy and goods, and in preventing anyone from impeding that open system. The failure of these states to develop as independent, efficient, well-managed, and self-governing transport corridors will leave control over this key Eurasian asset in the hands of either Russia, China, or Iran. Decisions taken – or not taken – today will shape this outcome for the long-term.

Let us then summarize the West's interests in the Caucasus and Central Asia:

- To foster the development of stable, sovereign and self-governing states, free from control by neighboring powers, and cooperating actively with Western governments and institutions in the spheres of economics, regional security, counter-terrorism, and conflict resolution.
- To put existing conflicts within the region on a path toward long-term and peaceful resolution, within the framework of international law, and with minimal manipulation by external powers.
- In a geographical environment that includes theocratic Iran as well as Iraq, the North Caucasus, Turkey, and Pakistan, for the Caucasus and Central Asia to be a zone of secular states with secular laws and courts, and modern secular education.
- To enable states of the region to evolve gradually but solidly into a zone of self-governing, law-based states that respect human rights, are free of corruption, and solicit and respond to citizens' interests and needs.
- To enable those countries and their citizens, to the extent they

wish to do so, to share Euro-Atlantic values in governance, information, education, culture, and human rights, and in such a way that they might serve as a model to neighbors and others elsewhere.

- To work with regional states to enable them to become suppliers of energy to Europe, thus diversifying the sources of Europe's energy supplies.
- For the Black Sea, Caucasus, and Caspian Sea to function as an unimpeded and reliable transit corridor by land, sea, and air between Europe/America and Central Asia, East Asia, and South Asia.
- For the same zone to become an important export-import corridor for the EU, China, and India not controlled by any of them but protected by all.

A CASE STUDY OF WESTERN FOREIGN RELATIONS

It is worth noting that western policies towards the region have been driven not by national leaders but primarily by the foreign policy bureaucracies of America and Europe. Top-level attention to these regions has generally been missing, but the exceptions should be noted: President George H. W. Bush involved himself directly in preparing the Partnership for Peace; President Bill Clinton and British Prime Minister Tony Blair took a direct interest in the development of the Baku-Tbilisi-Ceyhan pipeline; U.S. Defense Secretary Donald Rumsfeld interacted closely with Central Asian states following the 9/11 terrorist attacks; President George W. Bush took notice of the reforms that followed Georgia's 2003 revolution; and European leaders, primarily Nicolas Sarkozy, stepped up during and after the Russian war in Georgia, and EU institutions made efforts to develop a trans-Caspian Pipeline from Turkmenistan. Yet these engagements were rarely coordinated and never consistent. Especially since 2008, the voices of top level Western leaders has been weak or nonexistent in the formation of policy towards the region. This in turn has allowed the foreign policy bureaucracies to set the agenda and dictate the terms of Western policy. In this sense, this book is a case study of how large government structures in Europe and American interact, or fail to interact, in defining and carrying out their foreign relations.

Finally, let us note that the Caucasus and Central Asia provide a valuable case study of how the often divergent interests of Western policy relate to one another and how they can reinforce or contradict each other. At various times in the past quarter century Western powers have been intimately engaged in security affairs; economic and energy matters; and the promotion of democracy and human rights. This book will argue that these areas of interest are not inherently contradictory. Yet in practice, the lack of coordination and leadership in the development and implementation of policy has all too often caused it to appear that way. In the absence of clear directions from leaders, bureaucrats have engaged in turf wars, clashed over priorities, and allowed themselves to be influenced by special interests with narrow agendas. We can think of few world regions where these phenomena are as clearly and vividly manifested as in America's and Europe's relations with the Caucasus and Central Asia.

ENDNOTES

1. Eldar Ismailov and Vladimer Papava, *The Central Caucasus: Essays on Geopolitical Economy*, Stockholm: CA & C Press, 2006.
2. S. Frederick Starr, *In Defense of Greater Central Asia*, Washington: Central Asia-Caucasus Institute, Policy Paper, September 2008. (https://www.silkroadstudies.org/resources/pdf/SilkRoadPapers/2008_09_PP_Starr_Greater-Central-Asia.pdf)

SETTING THE SCENE: CENTRAL ASIA AND THE CAUCASUS, 1991–2016

■

Central Asia and the South Caucasus have undergone major changes in the twenty-five years since the USSR collapsed. This chapter sketches the region's development from independence to the present. It recalls the conditions under which these countries became independent, maps the achievements of the new states, and sets forth the key challenges to their further development.

CONDITIONS AT INDEPENDENCE

From 1989 onward, the western community devised a series of initiatives to guide the post-Communist countries in their process of "transition" toward liberal democracy. But that very notion of "transition" was based on the largely unstated assumption that all post-Communist countries were created equal – that their common Communist past meant they faced more or less the same challenges for the future. With the benefit of hindsight, it is clear that this assumption was faulty. In matters both tangible and intangible, the entities that had formed part of the Soviet Union were immeasurably less prepared for independent nationhood than their Eastern and Central European counterparts. As will be seen, the combination of the lack of meaningful experience of statehood and the higher level of integration that existed among Soviet republics severely complicated the building of statehood.

Nationhood

Prior to Soviet rule, the majority of the states of the region had never existed with the names or borders that they inherited in 1991. To be sure,

Armenia and Georgia had long established traditions of nationhood, and clearly defined national identities; Azerbaijan's emerged in the late nineteenth century. All three had prior histories of statehood, but their statehood harkened back to the medieval era, and those states had fragmented or dissolved long before the Russian conquest in the early nineteenth century. Only in 1918 did they re-emerge on the map. For almost three years, these three states struggled to establish themselves as members of the community of nations. Having spent their brief independence contesting each other's claims to territory, all three ultimately failed and were forcibly joined to the Soviet Union in 1920-21. When they regained independence seventy years later these old and unresolved conflicts over territory re-emerged. They continue to plague the South Caucasus today. But the experience of independence of 1918 created a foundation for the future. It is notable that both Azerbaijan and Georgia celebrate as their national day the establishment of statehood in May 1918, and not their independence from the Soviet Union.[1]

Central Asian states, however, did not have even such limited recent history of statehood to hark back to. All five republics were created by the Soviet leadership in the 1920s, and they bore little if any resemblance to any of the many and often powerful earlier states that had long existed in the region. Soviet planners created each entity around a titular nationality that was granted *pro forma* control over its state institutions. To this extent the Central Asian republics were not entirely artificial creations like many Middle Eastern states. But like those entities, they were created in an arbitrary fashion by faraway rulers who in many cases gave them boundaries that defied settlement patterns on the ground. This had evidently been the Soviet rulers' intention. This handicapped the new states when finally they gained independence, denying them elements of legitimacy that they then had to foster though deliberate policies that diverted attention from urgent economic and institutional reforms, including privatization and democratic development. This occurred not because the new governments ignored or failed to understand these matters, but because they had not only to build states but to define and mold the very *demos* that could form the basis for more participatory systems of government.

The legacy of Soviet thinking on issues of ethnicity and nationality did not help. While western societies embraced a citizenship-based concept of nationality and a constructivist understanding of ethnicity, Soviet thinkers did the opposite: they taught that nations, *ethnoses*, were primordial entities impermeable to change. Soviet law embodied and reinforced this notion. To change one's ethnic identity ('nationality' in Soviet parlance) was impossible, and the notion of dual nationality was nonexistent; children of mixed marriages were assigned one of the two ethnic identities. This meant that upon independence leaders found it difficult to consolidate new nations under a common civic identity, as so many post-colonial rulers have tried to do. To be sure, they launched inclusive terms like "Kyrgyzstani" or "Azerbaijani" to embrace all citizens. Georgia's President Saakashvili from 2004 onward struggled to redefine the traditionally highly ethnic-based Georgian identity as a civic identity for all inhabitants. But to varying degrees, the long populations themselves, and minority groups in particular, resisted such efforts.

Statehood

While challenges to the more abstract notion of nationhood were significant, those in the area of state-building were more dramatic. Indeed, it is here that the new states of Central Asia and the Caucasus differed most markedly from the East and Central European states. Having formed part of the Soviet Union, they were, in 1992, sovereign states only on paper. They lacked many of the key institutions that define statehood, had no demarcated boundaries, and weakly developed national economies.

The most glaring problem at independence was the absence of governing institutions. In the Soviet era, administrative power had been divided into three levels: central, republican and provincial. In spite of the formally federative nature of the USSR, the key political decisions were taken in Moscow. While the administrative structure of the union delegated authority to the republics, the Communist Party – where real power lay – was never decentralized. Meanwhile, responsibility for most "non-union" economic affairs rested to a considerable degree at the *oblast'* or provincial level; indeed, the surest way to rise to power for a Soviet-era official was to build a career in one of the regions. In other words, the institutions of the Soviet republics were undermined from both above and below. To be sure, the balance of power between the three levels changed over time. In the Brezhnev era, republican institutions had been fairly strong, with republican leaders allowed to run their republics as semi-independent fiefdoms. Gorbachev, however, in his efforts to modernize the Soviet Union, had worked hard to weaken republican institutions and concentrate power centrally. Independence therefore occurred at a time when republican institutions were deliberately being emasculated.

In the Caucasus and Tajikistan, the problem was compounded by the presence of several autonomous provinces and republics – territories where minority ethnic groups had been granted a special status in the

1920s. Not surprisingly, this status allowed local leaders to maintain a level of separation from the republic as a whole that would spur nationalism and separatism when the Union collapsed. It also gave Moscow a convenient tool to pressure these republics into submission. This was the root of the violent conflicts that began in Nagorno-Karabakh, Abkhazia, South Ossetia, and to a lesser extent in the Pamirs, and which, largely thanks to Russian interference, remain unresolved today.

The central executive, legislative and judiciary institutions of the Soviet era were all passed on to the new states. These continued to be plagued by Soviet ailments and needed to undergo fundamental reform in order to function in an independent state. Some institutions did not exist at all at the republican level, including the military, border guards, and ministries of foreign affairs. These needed to be created from scratch. They were often built on the remnants of Soviet institutions that had been located on the given republic's territory, and with personnel from Soviet institutions. Personnel, in fact, proved a major challenge. The authoritarian mentality and corrupt ways that had dominated Soviet government at all levels continued to make itself felt. The key logic of that outlook was that public office was gained through bribery or nepotism and held for the benefit not of the public but of the office-holder, his family, and his network. Political leaders could institute reforms, but they still had to deal with staffs that were unwilling or unable to adapt to new ways. It is no coincidence that the most well-functioning and progressive institutions across the region are those that were created from scratch after independence, allowing leadership to bring in younger staff who were less tainted by the Soviet past. The depth of this human resources problem is best illustrated by the decision by Georgian leaders after 2004 to adopt an Estonian model and simply pass over an entire generation of officials and hand bureaucratic posts to young western-trained officials who were less affected by the Soviet mentality. Georgia achieved remarkable results across the state bureaucracy but most regional states employed this tactic only in selected agencies of the state.

Economy and Infrastructure

The economy and infrastructure posed further challenges. The economies of former Soviet republics were far more closely tied to Moscow than were the "satellite" countries in Eastern Europe. In Central Asia and the Caucasus. Typically, they were commanded to produce raw materials for industrial centers that were primarily to the north and west. Similarly, transportation and communication infrastructures connected these republics to Moscow, but denied them connections to neighboring countries that historically had been their major trading partners. Therefore, Uzbekistan continues to market most of its cotton crop through the Baltic port of Riga, not the harbors on the Indian Ocean, though these are a thousand miles closer. The command economy had produced mainly goods that could not compete on the world market. Further, the new countries, all of them landlocked except for Georgia, had no way to get their goods efficiently to global markets, even if the products might otherwise have been competitive. When in rare instances they did, they found that their cost of production was higher than their competitors. As a result, the Central Asian and Caucasian landscape became littered with what became known as "Large Abandoned Objects" – failed Soviet-era enterprises that were simply abandoned until Chinese demand for metals caused their built infrastructure to be sold for scrap.[2]

The new borders further hampered the emergence of true national economies. Particularly in Central Asia, travel by road or rail between two points in a given country often required transit through a neighbor's territory – not once, but several times. This had not been a problem in the Soviet era, when borders between republics were administrative boundaries only. But upon independence travelers now had to cross international boundaries. Similarly, the region's energy infrastructure was not republican but regional. Central Asia's water resources – and therefore, hydropower facilities – are concentrated in the eastern mountains of Kyrgyzstan and Tajikistan. By contrast, the downstream countries – Kazakhstan, Turkmenistan and Uzbekistan – are rich in oil and natural gas. During the Soviet period the western republics shipped hydrocarbons east in winter, allowing the eastern republics to release water resources for irrigation downstream rather than hoard water to generate electricity. Upon independence, Kyrgyzstan and Tajikistan sought to continue this arrangement but met fierce resistance as the downstream countries sought to sell their hydrocarbons at world prices, at the same time considering water as a God-given and hence free resource. This led inevitably to the conflicts between upstream and downstream states over water that plague the region to this day.

This short overview makes it clear that at independence the challenges confronted by states in Central Asia and the Caucasus were of a different order of magnitude than their counterparts in Eastern and Central Europe. We will see how western policies, exacerbated this gap: Eastern and Central European states were showered with western development assistance and the prospect of membership in NATO and the European

Union. But the countries of Central Asia and the Caucasus, which received pennies on the dollar compared to countries further west, had no such prospects.

It was therefore entirely predictable that the transition to independence would be extremely painful across the region. The new governments had to deal simultaneously with building new state institutions, managing the fallout of the collapse of the Soviet economic system, and handling challenges to their newfound sovereignty. In most states, gross domestic product fell by half in the first three years of independence, a figure that was much higher in the countries affected by armed conflict – Armenia, Azerbaijan, Georgia, and Tajikistan. Poverty levels rose rapidly, and social, educational and health services verged on collapse. This prompted high levels of emigration, with lasting consequences for the population that remained. Rural areas were particularly hard hit, especially company towns where the large single employer had gone out of business. In the absence of a functioning economy and efficient state institutions, there emerged semi-feudal types of social organization. Important sectors of the economies and entire branches of government came under the influence of persons who were akin to medieval barons – heads of informal networks of power held together by common familial or regional identities or simple economic interest. These networks established themselves so strongly that in many countries they gained the ability to check the power of central governments. Paradoxically, the West treated these same governments as autocratic, often assuming that presidents had unlimited.[3]

Thus, Central Asia and the Caucasus faced an uphill battle in the 1990s. One form of social organization had collapsed and had been partly replaced by an even more strongly particularist form of government, and in a world where formally, the universalist norms of liberal democracy had declared victory. To this should be added yet another factor, this one psychological in nature. The West assumed that the rising generation of post-Soviet citizens would break psychologically from the soviet mold, and be ready to slip easily into new roles. While this might be true to a large extent in the Baltic states, it is manifestly not elsewhere, where the psychological legacy of Soviet styles of thought and habits of mind are proving more tenacious than expected.

ACHIEVEMENTS SINCE INDEPENDENCE

A visitor who experienced the collapse of the early 1990s would find, on a return visit twenty years later, that much of Central Asia and the Caucasus has changed beyond recognition. Such a visitor would find not only paved roads and regular access to water and electricity – all in short supply twenty years ago – but also, at least in capital cities, an urban middle class of well-dressed young people frequenting shops and cafés and who could guide the visitor in fluent English.

Even beyond such appearances, there is no doubt that the countries of Central Asia and the Caucasus have made important strides during the quarter century since independence. First and foremost, they have become real and functioning states that are recognized as such internationally. They have built viable state institutions and have, to a significant extent, worked to combat poverty. They have begun to build systems of modern education, and have maintained secular systems of laws and government. Finally, they have proven adroit at establishing themselves on the international scene and navigating between the great powers that surround them.

Statehood and Sovereignty

As we will see in the next section, the differences among the eight countries have grown tremendously since independence. Yet everywhere in the region governments succeeded in building sovereignty – that is, asserting the state's monopoly over the use of force, which is in itself no mean achievement. The experience of many post-colonial African countries shows the dangers of creating what political scientists have termed "shadow states," in which the state in the Weberian sense has practically ceased to exist. Similar centrifugal tendencies emerged in the early 1990s in the Caucasus and Central Asia, which became awash with rampant crime and a paramilitary groups. Yet the trend in Central Asia and the Caucasus has been resolutely toward the building of states with ever stronger, and in some cases even excessive, competencies. While that is a problem in itself, it is significant that the region has not experienced challenges to the integrity of states beyond those that existed at the time of independence. Those countries that were prone to internal strife – Azerbaijan, Georgia and Tajikistan – successfully halted the downward spiral toward disintegration, and successfully rebuilt the integrity of the state. In spite of regional and other differences, there has been no credible threat to statehood anywhere in the region. The only exception to this is the serious weakening of Kyrgyzstan in 2005-10, a period when the state was rocked by two violent changes of government and one bout of serious inter-ethnic strife in the country's south. But even there, and without significant assistance from abroad, Kyrgyzstan managed to survive as a sovereign entity and even to reinvent itself as Central Asia's only parliamentary republic.[4]

The countries of Central Asia and the Caucasus have also, for the most part, successfully established their external sovereignty, that is, established their independence in practice and not merely on paper. This was no small feat, considering that much of their security sector continued to be staffed by officials whose loyalties rested with intelligence headquarters in Moscow, and that Russian leaders continued to demand, formally or informally, a *droit de regard* over such key ministries as defense, interior and security. In Central Asia the process of building real independence was helped by Russia's weakness in the 1990s, which allowed regional countries some breathing room. But in the Caucasus, which Russian planners considered crucial to their immediate state interests, Moscow spent scarce resources to undermine statehood and secure its dominance even in the early 1990s, before it had reasserted its control over the Russian North Caucasus. Because of its conflict with Azerbaijan, Armenia chose in 1992 to align itself with Russia. In spite of heavy pressure, however, neither Azerbaijan nor Georgia followed suit. Quite the contrary, Russian interference strengthened their resolve to establish true independence and to reinforce it through alliances with the West. Today, less than a quarter of the population of either country supports a Russian orientation. Like Moldova, and Ukraine after 2014, these two countries paid a heavy price for this resolve: Moscow provided support for separatists that asserted control over a sixth of each country's territory, with the often explicit offer that this support would be subject to negotiation if Baku or Tbilisi changed their foreign policy orientation. Both refused to trade independence for territory.

In Central Asia, the three western states – Kazakhstan, Turkmenistan and Uzbekistan – benefited from their natural resource endowment to build independent foreign policies; by comparison, the smaller, poorer states to the east have struggled. Yet all five have sought to build what has come to be called "multi-vector" foreign policies, based on balancing their positive ties to Russia with equally positive ties to outside powers, including China, the United States, Europe, and other Asian powers. This notion was first formulated by Kazakhstan's long-time foreign minister, Kassym-Jomart Tokayev, who understood that Kazakhstan, given its unavoidable need to cooperate with Russia, could secure its independence only by building equally strong cooperation with China and the West. This quest for a positive balance between great powers explains much of Astana's seemingly hyper-active diplomacy since independence.[5] Given Kazakhstan's weakness at independence, its large population of ethnic Slavs, and its 4,000-mile land border with its former overlord, Kazakhstan's success at establishing its independence is remarkable. While Kazakhstan has been a member of all Russian-led efforts to integrate the former Soviet space, including the Eurasian Economic Union, it has worked with some success to limit this integration to the economic realm, rejecting all steps toward political union. By contrast, Turkmenistan and Uzbekistan have rejected – or in the latter case, abandoned[6] – all forms of economic and security integration with Moscow. Over time, these two states have managed significantly to reduce Moscow's ability to influence their internal affairs. Even Tajikistan, which has hosted a major Russian military presence since its civil war in the early 1990s, has so far succeeded in remaining outside the Eurasian Union project. Only Kyrgyzstan, following its two upheavals in 2005 and 2010, was sufficiently weakened to permit Russia to reassert its claims. In practice, this means that Russia can assert a *de facto* veto over Kyrgyzstan's foreign relations.

In sum, the states of Central Asia and the Caucasus have established themselves on the world scene and developed deep and comprehensive relations with outside powers in the economic, political, and military realms. In the Caucasus, western Europe and Turkey have proven the main counterbalance to Russian influence; in Central Asia, China has played that role. But while western analysts often discuss the regional states as pawns in a great game between large powers, it would be a serious mistake to underestimate the agency of these new and small states, in other words, their ability to withstand even very strong pressure from foreign powers and to navigate successfully between them in order to achieve their own goals. Only two states, Armenia and Kyrgyzstan, and each for their own reasons, have come perilously close to becoming client states. Yet even in these cases, there are limits to what Moscow can achieve.

A corollary to this is the regional countries' largely peaceful management of their mutual borders and of each other. With the exception of the Armenia-Azerbaijan conflict, there has been no serious military confrontation between the region's states. This is the more noteworthy because, as we have seen, their mutual borders were created colonially, with the deliberate intention to prevent ethnic and political consolidation. The map of the Ferghana Valley reflects the near-complete mismatch between topography, ethnic settlement patterns and international borders. Central Asia's most populated and most fertile region, home to a quarter of the region's population, is criss-crossed by borders and includes several "exclaves" – small islands of territory belonging to one state but surrounded by another. Managing these boundaries has led to considerable friction between Kyrgyzstan, Tajikistan and Uzbekistan, but for all their differences, they have managed their interactions in a largely peaceful manner.

Institution-Building

Central Asia and the Caucasus have gained renown for their informal politics and the continued prevalence of corruption. That said, the larger trend is toward the institutionalization of power. The near-anarchy of the early 1990s has given way to an improved stability and to the strengthening of governmental institutions, proving Mancur Olsen's assertion that "any individual who has autocratic control over a country will provide public goods to that country because he has an 'encompassing interest' in it".[7] Indeed, in Olson's vocabulary, a region that in the 1990s was replete with "roving bandits" now claims more "stationary bandits" with a stake in progress and stability. That does not mean the region has seen a trend toward greater political liberty or accountability. Yet the institutions run by informal power brokers are better managed and provide more public goods than a system based purely on confiscating the property of the citizenry. Stated differently, countries across the region have created an atmosphere more conducive to entrepreneurship and trade; this in turn has begun to generate the middle classes that will likely emerge as agents of political change down the road.

In the 1990s, all states of the region (with the partial exception of Turkmenistan) used international support to build the foundations of a modern state with basic laws and institutions. Aside from designing entirely new constitutions (which tended everywhere to build strong presidential systems of power) they also rewrote Soviet-era legal codes and undertook the reform of administrative institutions. Needless to say, while these institutions assuredly exist on paper, levels of implementation vary widely. But the states have all laid the groundwork for modern state institutions. Over time these new governing institutions have gained in experience and leverage. While most regional states retain presidential systems, Georgia and Kyrgyzstan have transitioned to parliamentary systems of government, and Armenia is in the process of doing so. Yet even in presidential systems, the parliaments have increasingly claimed a greater voice in national affairs in a way reminiscent of the slow rise of parliamentarism in nineteenth-century Europe. In 2017, both Kazakhstan and Uzbekistan shifted considerable powers from the presidency to the parliament.

The growing importance of institutions can be seen in the thorny issue of succession. Succession is the weak point of any authoritarian system; yet the record in Central Asia and the Caucasus suggests it is like Conan Doyle's proverbial "dog that did not bark." Fifteen years ago, analysts predicted the likely chaos from anticipated successions' in Azerbaijan and Georgia, both ruled by septuagenarian strongmen. Yet while the two countries saw dramatically divergent successions in 2003, both accomplished them without major disturbances. The same was true in Turkmenistan in 2006. Georgia managed a highly contested transfer of power in 2012 that even involved a period of French-style "cohabitation" between opposing political forces. The Uzbek transition following the death of Islam Karimov in 2016 was similarly smooth. As such, the violent overthrow of the Akayev government in Kyrgyzstan in 2005 and of the Bakiev regime in 2010 stand out as exceptions. Kazakhstan, too, has designed elaborate, constitutional mechanisms for succession centering on the upper chamber of parliament.

International Financial Institutions helped the countries with macroeconomic stabilization programs in the 1990s, which laid the groundwork for modern economies everywhere. This involved the disorienting transition to a market economy, the introduction of private property, and the privatization of large, medium, and small enterprises. All countries launched their national currencies, which have proven relatively stable, though considerable fluctuations have resulted from swings in the price of oil and the devaluations in Russia. As a result, the International Monetary Fund has concluded that all countries in the region have a realistic chance of transitioning into middle-income economies by 2050.

Secular Governance, Laws and Education

It is important to note that the countries of Central Asia and the Caucasus include fully half of the world's secular Muslim-majority states. Indeed, the role of religion in politics is incomparably larger in the governing of Christian Armenia and Georgia than in any of the Muslim-majority countries.

Secularism, of course, was forcibly introduced in the form of Soviet atheism in the last century. Yet it also had local roots, as the Muslims of the Russia empire were among the first to produce secularly-oriented intellectuals in the late nineteenth century. But while all six Muslim-majority states in the region discarded official atheism and took steps to provide for religious freedom, all six states in fact transitioned to a model of modern secularism that should more correctly be termed *laïcité*, inspired by the French and (pre-Erdoğan) Turkish models. Under this model, as opposed to Anglo-Saxon forms of secularism, the primary aim is not to ensure individual freedom of religion but to protect the state and citizenry from undue religious influence. Everywhere in the region there is in fact less separation of Church and state than the subordination of religion to the state. The states, in fact, take pride in endorsing traditional organized religions and are wary of any new religious influences – whether in the form of Christian missionaries or Salafi preachers. Meanwhile, the states aggressively promote inter-religious coexistence and harmony, exemplified by frequent displays at home and abroad of the collegial relationships among diverse religious leaders, including Jewish rabbis. Unlike anywhere else in the Muslim world, high governmental officials make a point out of being seen with Jewish community leaders, thereby sending a powerful signal to society that anti-Semitism is unacceptable. It should therefore be no surprise that Jewish organizations in Israel and the West have formed close and positive relations with governments everywhere in the region.

During the 1990s, the education sector was in shambles across the region. With the economic collapse, the physical infrastructure of schools fell into disrepair, and teachers no longer received living wages. Growing poverty also meant that especially in rural areas and particularly for girls school attendance at the secondary level began to decline precipitously. As in other sectors of society, a system of informal payments arose, forcing parents to pay teachers for students' passage to the next grade and for diplomas. While many of these problems have yet to be fully addressed, governments across the region fully recognized the importance of modern secular education, and worked to build a new generation of secular elites. In several countries, notably Kazakhstan with its *Bolashak* program as well as Uzbekistan and Azerbaijan, with their support for students to study abroad, governments enabled thousands of students to study abroad. Georgia and Armenia lacked the funds to pay for such large-scale programs, but European and American programs like the Muskie fellowships made it possible for hundreds of aspiring young professionals from both countries (as well as other countries in the region) to obtain modern Western educations. By the 2000s, several governments began to address the need to build quality tertiary education at home. Azerbaijan and Kazakhstan took the lead by establishing the ADA and Nazarbayev Universities, created in partnership with western experts, teaching in English, relying to a considerable extent on western professors, and operating in a fully transparent manner. Turkmenistan meanwhile established a new International University with teaching in English. Other states have focused on reforming existing institutions, sometimes with positive results, as at the Tashkent Technical University. Meanwhile, Western and Turkish private donors have added to the educational resources of the region by establishing numerous new independent universities. Uzbekistan meanwhile set up a large network of vocational-technical high schools. While much remains to be done in the realm of primary and secondary education, the avenues for obtaining a high-quality secular education are gradually improving across the region.

INCREASINGLY DIFFERENT

To a greater or lesser extent, all of these initiatives are manifested across all Central Asia and the Caucasus. But it is also obvious that the eight countries have grown increasingly different from one another. Thus, thanks to their shared Soviet heritage, Georgia and Tajikistan in 1991 shared certain similarities, but they have very little in common today. The differences between the countries are visible in many areas. The most obvious divide is economic, between resource-rich and resource-poor countries. This division intersects with the political differences between the more liberal and the more authoritarian states, as well as with the diverging degree of political independence of the countries. Roughly speaking, the resource-rich countries tend to be more authoritarian but also more independent; while the resource-poor states tend to be more liberal but also weaker players on the international scene. To be sure, there are important exceptions to this generalization, which we shall address shortly.

Resource-rich vs resource-poor countries

When discussing the economic development of Central Asia and the Caucasus, international financial institutions no longer attempt to view the region as a single entity. Rather, they divide the states according to one simple variable: whether they import or export oil, which corresponds to the growing divide between richer and poorer countries in the region. The region comprises four states exporting oil and gas – Azerbaijan, Kazakhstan, Turkmenistan and Uzbekistan – and four importers – Armenia, Georgia, Kyrgyzstan and Tajikistan. Over twenty-five years, these groups of countries have become increasingly different from each other, with their diverging economic structures exerting a powerful influence on their political systems and foreign policy.

Political scientists have argued convincingly that reliance on hydrocarbons, or any single natural resource, constitutes a "resource curse." Elements of this are visible across the region. Large fluctuations in the oil price in the past decade has seen leaders of Azerbaijan and Kazakhstan scramble to adjust their currencies and budgets. Yet there is no denying that citizens in oil-exporting countries across the region are better off than their resource-poor counterparts. The distinction is most apparent also in the area of poverty alleviation. Azerbaijan and Kazakhstan have made remarkable advances, reducing poverty levels to around five percent. By contrast, Georgia and Kyrgyzstan have seen little change since independence, poverty levels remaining at 20 percent and 30 percent, respectively, in spite of billions of dollars in development aid to these countries.

Thanks both to the Soviet heritage and the landlocked character of all but one of the regional states, no country of the region has moved beyond the role of a provider of raw materials, be it oil, gold, cotton or foodstuffs. Oil and gas have driven the regional states' integration into the world economy. This began with the construction of the Baku-Ceyhan oil pipeline in the late 1990s onward, and was followed some years later by the Turkmen and Kazakh gas export pipelines to China. Only after this did the focus begin to turn to the development of rail and road links that could benefit other sectors of the economy.

This divergence matters greatly in terms of politics. Rents from hydrocarbons enable governments to increase public spending, co-opt elites, and provide relative stability. As will be seen, rents also enable governments to build stronger security institutions, thus making the resource-rich countries evolve in an authoritarian direction whereas poorer countries have proven more amenable to participatory politics. However, in times of low oil prices the resource-rich countries have had trouble reducing the public spending that the population has come to take for granted, in spite of the fact that they have sovereign wealth funds that were designed to cushion such shocks. It is no coincidence that social unrest in the region has been concentrated in the resource-poor states, particularly Georgia, Kyrgyzstan and Tajikistan. Resource-rich countries also have the ability to protect their independence more effectively by building stronger institutions to withstand foreign subversion. By contrast, poorer countries cannot match the financial ability of foreign powers to foment and co-opt oppositional movements and the governments themselves. Countries like Armenia and Kyrgyzstan, but also Georgia and Tajikistan, have been groping to manage Russian economic warfare designed to undermine their economies and to acquire their key economic assets in exchange for debt relief.

Political Systems

Notwithstanding the fact that they were all part of the same political system down to 1991, the eight countries of the region have developed widely diverse political systems. The main trend across the region has been the consolidation of authoritarian forms of government. That should come as no surprise, given the authoritarian character of the four major powers surrounding the region: Russia, China, Iran and Turkey. And in light of the low and falling level of American and European presence in most of the region, it would have been surprising if the surrounding authoritarian environment did not influence the countries of Central Asia and the Caucasus and help justify their evolution in the direction of authoritarianism.

There are important divergences among the authoritarian states, both in terms of the level of political and economic freedom they allow, and in the forms of informal government that exists behind the scenes. Azerbaijan and Kazakhstan provide a modicum of political freedoms, allowing opposition movements and media and a relatively free internet. Uzbekistan and Tajikistan have tended toward greater authoritarianism, as has Turkmenistan. Yet the informal powers of the presidents, and of the coalition upon which they built their power, differs greatly. Many observers ignore the fact that the level of personal control exercised by the chief executive does not necessarily make a country more or less authoritarian. Thus, Kazakhstan's President probably concentrates the greatest amount of personal power in the region, with the possible exception of Turkmenistan, while in Azerbaijan and Uzbekistan presidents are more correctly described as *primus inter pares* in a complex and sophisticated balance of power between elite factions. The roles of members of the presidents' families and of regional elites are visible everywhere in the region, but most leaders have worked to broaden their coalition by building bridges to other elite groups. One state, Tajikistan, has gone in the other direction, concentrating increasing power over time in the President's family and native region of Kulyab. Similarly, in Armenia, elite groups hailing from Nagorno-Karabakh remain dominant.

Two countries in the region – Georgia and Kyrgyzstan – have bucked the trend by replacing presidential systems with parliamentary forms of government. They have also seen transitions of power through elections, in 2012 and 2015, respectively, that have contributed to reduce the political instability and polarization that these countries experienced earlier. Like many emerging democracies, however, their political institutions remain weak, and formal institutions of power are at risk of falling under the control of informal power brokers. In Georgia, business tycoon Bidzina Ivanishvili, the winner of the 2012 elections, continues to run the country though he resigned from politics after a year as prime minister. The 2016 election, in which he did not formally run, only strengthened his informal control.

Levels of Sovereignty

Twenty-five years ago, the eight republics of Central Asia and the Caucasus were mere administrative entities of the Soviet Union. Only those in the South Caucasus experienced significant popular movements for self-rule or independence. Even though Kazakhs mounted major demonstrations against rule by Russians in 1986, in most of Central Asia such forces were marginal when the Union collapsed. That did not prevent leaders in all states from seeking to maximize their independence subsequently. But their levels of success have varied greatly, mainly reflecting their degree of economic independence. Several of the poorer states of the region have struggled to assert their sovereignty. Armenia and Kyrgyzstan in particular have come to rely on an increasingly deep and unequal economic and political relationship with Russia. This has reached such an extent that it now threatens their sovereignty by reducing the ability of the leadership of each country to make key decisions independently. Moscow has sought to exert similar pressure on Tajikistan and Georgia, with less success. Tajikistan continues to eschew membership in the Eurasian Union. Moscow's efforts to subdue the more openly independent-minded Georgia led to a military invasion in 2008, which nevertheless failed to alter Georgia's determination to seek integration with the West. Among the energy-exporting states, Kazakhstan stands out by its active membership in Russian-led integration schemes. As noted above, this is a reflection of Kazakhstan's political, demographic and geographic realities, and of President Nazarbayev's long-standing personal enthusiasm for economic cooperation and integration of all sorts. Nevertheless, compared to its weakness at independence, Kazakhstan has developed an impressive level of sovereignty, expressed and reinforced by its activism on the international scene.

Azerbaijan, Turkmenistan and Uzbekistan stand out for their dogged ability to defend their sovereignty and independence while avoiding direct confrontations with Moscow. All three states have experienced the effects of Russia's subversive activities on their soil and are extremely wary of Russian integration mechanisms. Azerbaijan, moreover, finds itself in a military standoff with Armenia, a key Russian ally. Yet in spite of these problems, all three states have succeeded in establishing relations of mutual respect with the Russian leadership, relations considerably more equal than those of their smaller neighbors.

SERIOUS ISSUES REMAINING

Having cataloged the noteworthy accomplishments of the states of Central Asia and the Caucasus in the quarter century since their independence, it is appropriate to discuss also the numerous serious issues that remain unresolved. Primary among these are the need to overcome the Soviet legacy in all its forms and to address problems caused by the region's landlocked nature. A third challenge is to improve the quality of governance, while a fourth is to broaden, internationalize, and deepen sources of news and information. Finally, of course, there is the vexing problem of relations with Russia.

Overcoming Landlockedness
With the exception of Georgia, all countries of Central Asia and the Caucasus are landlocked. They are part of a growing trend: while less than ten countries in the world were landlocked prior to the twentieth century, many of the states created in the late twentieth century suffer from this liability. These now constitute a fifth of the world's states. Being landlocked has direct and very tangible consequences in the economic realm. As early as 1776 the British economist Adam Smith observed that the costs and difficulty of transportation exact a high toll on landlocked areas, pointing specifically to the comparative lack of development of inner Asia and Africa.[8] Today's economists have concluded that the average value of landlocked countries' exports is half that of other states, and their transport costs 50 percent greater.[9] The only highly developed landlocked states are in Western Europe, where they benefit from well-developed infrastructure and a high level of economic integration, which effectively neutralize their landlocked nature.[10]

Such is not the reality in Central Asia which, together with South Asia, has been dubbed the least connected region in the world. Political, geographical and infrastructural factors continue to prevent the development of effective communications in the region. The first challenge is distance: from the Ferghana valley, the greatest population center of the region, to the Indian Ocean is a mere 1,100 miles. But since communications through Afghanistan have been cut for a century, the closest sea ports to which the valley is connected are Riga, 2,300 miles distant, and Shanghai, 2,800 miles away. Poti, in Georgia, is only 1,500 miles away, but remains inaccessible. Iran's new port at Chabahar holds important possibilities, and Pakistan's new port at Gwadar offers even more promise. But connections to Chabahar have yet to be constructed and links to Gwadar remain for now a mere dream. To make matters worse, seventy years of Soviet rule meant that the transportation and communication infrastructure everywhere in the region was oriented toward Moscow, while international connections to the east, south and west were poor or non-existent. Finally, the erection of national boundaries within the region hurt what economic integration existed, further discouraging trade. Problems of governance have added significant tolls in terms of fees, informal payments and wait times at borders.

Overcoming landlockedness will require modern infrastructure and improved governance, but the answer lies not only in finding improved access to the high seas. In fact, what once made Central Asia and the Caucasus developed civilizations was the primacy of overland trade. Today both external powers and the region's states have embraced the notion of rebuilding land corridors connecting Europe and Asia across this broad landmass. Shipments of freight between coastal areas of Europe and Asia are now carried out either by air or sea, leaving a considerable niche for land routes that are cheaper than air freight, but much faster than shipping by sea. The attractiveness of the land route will undoubtedly be even stronger for inland areas such as eastern Europe, northern India, or western China.

Information

Closely connected to the problems of transportation and communication is the field of information. Central Asia and the Caucasus are landlocked not only economically but, in a sense, also mentally. Not being situated "on the way" to anywhere, their development of information links to the rest of the world has been excruciatingly slow. While government control over information is one piece of the problem, it is by no means the only one. Moscow's continued domination of Russian-language media broadcast across the region is an important impediment to the development of a freer information landscape. For now, citizens of the region form opinions on world events mainly from government-controlled or Russian news sources. Since these are packaged in a more attractive way than in the Soviet era, the ability of new sources, from the West and elsewhere, including the radio stations financed by the U.S. government, to reach larger audiences are limited.

Governance

While regional countries have built new governmental institutions in the past quarter century, the quality of governance across the region leaves much to be desired. Authoritative indexes of corruption indicate that the countries of Central Asia and the Caucasus are among the poorer performers globally. Aside from administrative corruption, citizens of the region are confronted with legal systems that they do not trust to uphold their rights, as well as authorities who often appear to exercise power in an arbitrary manner. It goes without saying that public dissent in many of the countries is fraught with risk, and the avenues for oppositional politics very circumscribed. To make matters worse, the tradition of voluntary organizations is relatively weak, something that foreign donors have sought to remedy by funding non-government organizations. Unfortunately, as will be seen later in this study, these have tended to be more responsive to the funding opportunities in western capitals than to their own grassroots or national needs.

While they are correctly described as authoritarian, most of the region's countries are in fact under-governed. On paper, much power is concentrated in state institutions. But in reality these institutions often function poorly. One of the chief problems remains the dominance of informal politics over institutions, and the personalization of power. In fact, with the benefit of hindsight it is clear that the political transition that regional states carried out in 1991 was not the one envisaged by the reigning western transition paradigm. When the authoritarian and corrupt Soviet administrative system collapsed it was not replaced by the kind of embryonic liberal democratic system that emerged in Central Europe. Instead, the power vacuum in Central Asia and the Caucasus allowed power-brokers who sat on top of powerful state institutions to privatize them. In each state, various coalitions of power-brokers were built, based on regional or ethnic origin, family connections, or pure economic interest. During the 1990s, precisely because the political transition was accompanied by an all-encompassing economic transition that included the introduction of private property, these informal coalitions were able to consolidate their staying power. When state-owned enterprises were privatized, it was the existing political power-brokers who were best positioned to appropriate the assets. At the same time, those who controlled state institutions that interacted directly with citizens – such as police, customs, courts, and even education and health – implemented a system based on informal fees that citizens were forced to pay in exchange for the delivery of services or the avoidance of sanctions. In the typical case, a citizen would pay a police officer to avoid being fined for a real or imaginary offense. The officer would in turn pass on a set amount to his superior, and so on up to the minister. This created a system reminiscent of medieval Europe's feudal order, with power-brokers across Central Asia and the Caucasus cast in the role of feudal barons. Like the feudal order, this system proved highly resilient, not least because of the substantial financial power it concentrated in the hands of those at the top of the system. This arrangement endures today, although (as already noted) the more prudent 'barons' are transitioning from the role of "roving bandits" to that of "stationary bandits."

It is worth noting that this system, inexorably connected with bad governance, was worst in the more liberal states, like Georgia or Kyrgyzstan, where the authoritarian hierarchy was relatively weak. Of course, this type of system survives only when the division of competencies among the 'barons' is acceptable to the key actors. This is often the case in the more authoritarian systems. But in the more liberal ones, the chief executive proved unable to rein in the 'barons' or keep them from fighting each other, which often resulted in anarchic corruption and a collapse of public services. This is what caused the revolutions in Georgia and Kyrgyzstan. In oil-producing countries, governments could use rents from oil to lessen the cost of public services or grease the system, alleviating the burden on citizens.

Westerners would term this pattern of behavior simply "corruption". But in fact, it is tantamount to an alternative form of social organization – what political scientists would call a particularist rather than universalist political system. To varying degrees, this remains the case across Central Asia and the Caucasus. Only one country, Georgia, was able to break the back of this system through an aggressive reform program that first abolished the offending state institutions and then rebuilt them from scratch. Experience in many other countries suggests that building new institutions is incomparably easier than reforming corrupt ones.

The Legacy of the Soviet Mentality
Down to 1991 it was widely understood that the Soviet government had devoted immense energy and resources to shaping the mentality of the peoples of the USSR. However, in the generation before the collapse of the USSR western observers were fascinated not by the successes of these efforts but by their failure, thanks to which, it was argued, an entire rising generation had emerged with open mentalities that were unfettered by Soviet ideology. After 1991 it was assumed that these people would be in charge of the post-Soviet states.

What this analysis missed is that the daily practices of a corrupted state-owned and state-run economy and of enterprises fully controlled by central planners had created a mentality that permeated not only the old regime but many of its critics as well and, equally, the public at large. This mentality has persisted throughout the former Soviet-ruled states, not least in the Caucasus and Central Asia. Its hallmarks are a reluctance to take publicly visible initiatives, a readiness to resort to corrupt initiatives and practices, and a general passivity with respect to civic activity, until such a time that frustration explodes in unfocused opposition. To date this psychological 'hangover' from Soviet times has barely been acknowledged, let alone addressed.

The Russia Problem

Beginning with the United States in 1776, the post-colonial world has been seriously concerned over its relationship to the former colonial powers. In Central Asia and the Caucasus that problem is compounded by two realities: first, that its former colonial overlord is adjacent to them and not overseas; and second, that it is not a western democracy but a committed revisionist power. Thus, Russia's trajectory from a troubled country in the 1990s that sought integration with Europe to Putin's self-conscious and anti-western regime seeking to rebuild something akin to the Soviet empire.

We have noted how the various countries of the region have adopted widely varied methods for dealing with this challenge, with mixed results. But they all face what is essentially an existential threat to their sovereignty. Putin's agenda, implemented directly in bilateral relations as well as through cooperative structures, lies squarely in the reduction of the sovereignty of the region's states and their subordination to Moscow, in fact if not in law. In practice, the region has long suffered from the impact of what western analysts have belatedly termed Russia's "hybrid warfare" – a mobilization of various instruments of statecraft, overt as well as covert, to divide and rule.

Addressing this threat has everywhere become a chief concern for political leaders, whether or not they acknowledge it openly. And given the gravity of the threat, it has also created incentive structures directly at odds with western normative interests: to the leader of any regional state, the instinctive response to the hybrid threat posed by Moscow is to strengthen control over state and society, not loosen it as proposed by western advocates of democracy. Furthermore, Moscow's overt disdain for democratic governance means that to engage in liberalization not only opens up the state to Russian subversion but also attracts Moscow's ire, as shown by its actions toward Georgia and subsequently Ukraine. In sum, the Russian challenge has led to a securitization of many spheres of life in the region, from its politics and economy to civil society, that has been detrimental to normal political reform and progress. Unfortunately, American and European leaders have gravely underestimated this challenge, and continue to preach that democratization is the best guarantee for security, without providing an engagement in the security sphere that would lend credence to their admonitions.

A Challenging Regional Environment

Aside from developments in Russia, the international environment in the areas surrounding Central Asia and the Caucasus has deteriorated in the past decade. The common perception across the region is that America and Europe, but particularly the U.S., have disengaged from its affairs. This is compounded by the broader decline of the Muslim world, of which most of the region is a part. Developments in Afghanistan, Iran, the Middle East and Turkey have a direct and largely negative impact on Central Asia and the Caucasus. The continued unrest in Afghanistan and unpredictability of that country's future keeps Central Asia on edge, knowing that Afghanistan has in the recent past exported Islamic radicalism into the region. At the same time, Central Asians are quick to acknowledge that a positive future for Afghanistan is crucial to the region's prospects for trading with South Asia and beyond. Iran's international behavior is of concern to the Caucasus, where Azerbaijan is exposed to Iranian ambitions of hegemony. But this pales in comparison to the collapse of Iraq and Syria, and the emergence there of the Islamic State. While relatively limited numbers of Central Asians and Caucasians have joined ISIS, the expansion of that organization into the North Caucasus and Afghanistan is being watched with grave concern by all secular governments in the region. Finally, the decline of Turkey is of immense symbolic importance for a region whose majority is Turkic-speaking. Once a model of secular governance and integration with the West, a Turkey that is descending into instability and Islamist-tinged authoritarianism leaves the region's states increasingly isolated. One could add to this list concerns over China's long-term ambitions in the region although Chinese policies to date have largely benefited Central Asia, and especially its efforts to escape Russian hegemony. All in all, Central Asia and the Caucasus see their international environment as considerably more volatile today than at any time since independence, a reality that is not helpful for the emergence of stable, secular and democratic societies there.

CONCLUSION

The nations of Central Asia and the Caucasus have come a long way since independence. At the same time, they continue to face very real challenges to their security and development – some of their own making, and others that they can only affect on the margins. As we turn to western policies toward the region, one conclusion must be stressed repeatedly: western leaders and analysts alike have grossly underestimated the challenges to the development of modern democratic statehood across this region. As a result, the U.S. and Europe also underestimate what the countries have in fact accomplished without unleashing social strife, and have been overly impatient with their slow progress toward better and more open governance and hence ineffective in assisting them in that process.

ENDNOTES

1. Armenia celebrates this date as Republic Day, but has as its national day the declaration of independence in September 1991.
2. Wendell Steavenson, *Stories I Stole*, Grover Press, 2004, p. 93.
3. S. F. Starr, Clans, *Authoritarian Rulers, and Parliaments in Central Asia*, Washington: Central Asia-Caucasus Institute & Silk Road Studies Program, Silk Road Paper, 2006. (http://www.silkroadstudies.org/resources/pdf/SilkRoadPapers/2006_06_SRP_Starr_Clans.pdf)
4. Shirin Akiner, *Kyrgyzstan 2010: Conflict and Context*, Silk Road Paper, Central Asia-Caucasus Institute & Silk Road Studies Program, July 2016. (http://silkroadstudies.org/publications/silkroad-papers-and-monographs/item/13207)
5. Johan Engvall and Svante E. Cornell, *Asserting Statehood: Kazakhstan's Role in International Organizations*, Silk Road Paper, Central Asia-Caucasus Institute & Silk Road Studies Program, December 2015. (http://silkroadstudies.org/resources/pdf/SilkRoadPapers/2015_12_SRP_Statehood.pdf)
6. Uzbekistan joined the Eurasian Economic Community (Eurasec) in 2006, but suspended its participation in 2008. It joined the Collective Security Treaty Organization in 2006, but withdrew in 2012.
7. Mancur Olsen, "Dicatorship, Democracy and Development", *American Political Science Review*, vol. 87 no. 3, 1993, p. 567.
8. Adam Smith, *The Wealth of Nations*, in The Glasgow Edition of the Works and correspondence of Adam Smith, Oxford university Press, 1976, vol. 2, pp. 35-36.
9. Brenda Shaffer and Avinoam Idan, "Locked Out", *Foreign Policy*, February 4, 2014. (http://foreignpolicy.com/2014/02/04/locked-out/)
10. Michael L. Faye et. al., "The Challenges Facing Landlocked Developing Countries", *Journal of Human Development*, vol. 5 no. 1, March 2004, 31-68.

WESTERN ACTIVITY AND ACHIEVEMENTS IN THE CAUCASUS AND CENTRAL ASIA

Neither the United States nor Europe was prepared to deal with the independent states brought into being by the collapse of the USSR. During Soviet times both had managed their limited contacts with non-Russian republics overwhelmingly through Moscow. Even though the combined populations of the independent states of the Caucasus and Central Asia total 60% of the Russian Republic's population, Western governments lacked people who knew their languages, cultures, and social systems. Of necessity, they left the management of relations with the Caucasus and Central Asia mainly in the hands of Russianists who were dependent on Russian sources of information. This situation has since changed for the better, but it long contributed to a certain distortion of policy – the same kind of distortion that would have existed in the late eighteenth century had Europeans persisted in viewing the newly independent United States mainly through British eyes and British sources.

In spite of the surprise with which they greeted the collapse of the Soviet Union, the U.S. and Europe have in twenty-five years made significant contributions to the Caucasus and Central Asia. They organized their relations with the regional states largely on the basis of the "baskets" of issues identified in the 1975 Helsinki Final Act, which carried certain built-in problems. Yet as this chapter will show, Western powers contributed very significantly to securing the sovereignty and independence of these states. They took a direct interest in their security and the resolution of conflicts and played a critical role in bringing their most valuable assets – oil and natural gas – to markets.

Western governments also provided considerable sums for humanitarian and development assistance, though the fruits of this assistance are mixed. Finally, but with an even spottier record, western powers contributed to the development of democratic institutions in the region.

PHASES OF RELATIONS

Relations between the U.S. and Europe, on one hand, and Central Asia and the Caucasus, on the other, can be divided into three phases. In a first phase, which lasted from late 1991 to the September 11, 2001, terrorist attacks, the West became conscious of the emerging region and established constructive relations in a variety of fields. A second stage ran from 2001 to 2008, during which the EU became more active, investments in the energy sphere came to fruition, but in which the region increasingly came to be viewed through the prism of the war in Afghanistan. The third phase began in the fall of 2008 with the Russian-Georgian war and the financial crisis. It has seen an aggressive Russian attempt to reassert its power and a certain disengagement by the West, particularly the United States.

Discovering Central Asia and the Caucasus, 1991-2001

During the first phase, the U.S. and European nations were quick to recognize the new states and to issue declarations supportive of their sovereignty and peaceful development. American embassies were quickly established throughout the region, but only the largest European countries were to maintain embassies in every country of the region. On July 2, 1992, the U.S. Congress passed the Freedom for Russia and Emerging Eurasian Democracies and Open Markets Support Act (FSA, HR 282). Known as the "Freedom Support Act," this legislation defined and organized the official U.S. response to the collapse of the USSR and its future relations with the twelve so-called "newly Independent states" formed by the former Soviet republics. The following year the EU signed a Multilateral Agreement on International Transport for the development of transport initiatives between the EU, the Caucasus and Central Asia. Named TRACECA, the initiative inaugurated a Permanent Secretariat in February 2001. Visionary in concept, in that it accurately foresaw the possibility of transforming transport between Asia and Europe, TRACECA long remained underfunded, yet it persisted and eventually accomplished most of its agenda of projects. Throughout the 1990s, individual members of the European Union extended emergency relief and development assistance to both regions through active programs coordinated by the EU. Great Britain, the Netherlands, and Sweden were particularly active, as was non-EU member Switzerland, which focused its aid mainly on mountainous countries.

USAID assumed responsibility for most, but not all, U.S. aid and assistance programs in both regions. Even while the Freedom Support Act was still being drafted, USAID moved briskly to establish a new "eastern Europe" unit and to concentrate its attention on three main areas. The three foci, or "Transitions," as USAID termed them, broadly corresponded to the three Helsinki "baskets," with one addressing the transition to market economies, a second dealing with the social sector, especially health and education, and the third covering the development of more open, effective, and democratic governments. The latter substituted for the Helsinki "security" basket, which was understood to be the responsibility of the Pentagon. Billions of dollars were allocated and spent on a welter of new programs in diverse spheres that were established throughout the region. Thousands of Americans and large numbers of locals participated actively in their implementation. This phase lasted down to the end of the 1990s. In Europe, by contrast, the start was slower, but programs of EU member states rapidly gained momentum and support.

During this first phase of relations, economic ties between Western countries and the region also developed. The main interactions were investments to extract raw materials. Indeed, Western multinational corporations had taken an interest in the oil and gas resources of the Soviet Union even before it collapsed in 1991. Following independence, new opportunities emerged: the new poor but energy-rich states were desperate to bring these resources to market, but could not do so on their own. This resulted in their offering partnerships under very favorable conditions to the oil multinationals. Production Sharing Agreements provided considerable cash transfers to the governments at signing, but had revenue sharing schemes that allowed the multinationals not only to control portions of the resources but to recoup their investment relatively quickly. As Exxon, Chevron, Amoco, BP, Statoil, and others acquired assets in Azerbaijan and Kazakhstan, and sought fields in Turkmenistan, they were supported increasingly by their governments, which had meanwhile developed bilateral relations with the host governments.

In sum, during this period, relations developed in several areas – security, economic cooperation, and governance issues – with neither of these issue areas taking precedence over the other. While there were sins of omission, discussed in the next chapter, relations between the West and the region started out on a solid footing.

Coming to Fruition but Losing Focus: 2001-2008

Relations entered a second phase following the September 11,

2001, terrorist attacks on New York and Washington. It brought greatly intensified interaction between the West and the region, not only in security but also in energy. It also saw the EU taking a more serious approach to the region and a political transformation in Georgia that attracted unprecedented attention to that country. Yet the seeds of trouble that had been planted earlier now began to sprout. This occurred in part because the U.S.'s "freedom agenda" led it increasingly to divide regional countries into good and bad performers as measured by Washington's scale of democratization, and in part because both Washington and Brussels came to view much of the region in the narrow context of the pacification and development of Afghanistan.

9/11 caused America and its NATO allies to fight a war in the heart of the Eurasian continent, thousands of miles from the closest western military facility. The war effort would not have been possible without the cooperation of the states of Central Asia, which provided basing rights as well as logistical support, and of the Caucasus, which provided a narrow transport corridor to Afghanistan that neither Russia nor Iran dared shut down. This brought considerable American attention to the region and gave it a stake in the stability and development of these countries. Counter-terrorism for a time became the cornerstone of relations, although this did not mean other areas were forgotten. Indeed, the period saw the long-time Western investment in the region's energy sector come to fruition, with the construction of a pipeline infrastructure capable of delivering Caspian oil and gas to European markets. It also saw acrimony over human rights issues.

The 2003 Rose Revolution in Georgia was a landmark event, launched and driven by local leaders but facilitated by the close attention the U.S. paid to the country's unruly politics. It proved that political reform in a post-Soviet state outside the Baltic region was possible. It also coincided with the appearance of the Bush administration's "Freedom Agenda" and appeared to justify it. Garnering great support in America, the Rose Revolution caused Georgia to be the first, and so far the only, country in the region to receive a U.S. presidential visit, which occurred in 2005.

During this period, both the EU and NATO took more active institutional roles in the region, reaching out to it with a number of new programs and initiatives. Not only did this reflect and in turn stimulate western engagement, but it created a new role for those states of Central and Eastern Europe that had formerly lived under Communism and were in a better position than other Europeans to understand and engage with Central Asia and the Caucasus. The South Caucasus was officially included in the EU's Neighborhood Policy in 2004, while in 2007 the EU developed its first strategy for Central Asia. NATO, through its highly innovative Partnership for Peace program, became deeply engaged with countries throughout the region. Georgia (like Ukraine) came to view full NATO membership as the keystone of its security, but this aspiration was not welcomed by a majority of NATO members.

The introduction of the Freedom Agenda, however, occurred just as a more authoritarian regime was consolidating its control in Moscow. Vladimir Putin and his colleagues viewed what they called "color revolutions," i.e., the spread of democracy, as an existential threat to themselves. This inserted a powerful ideological element into the *realpolitik* of the region. When western powers began to prioritize relations with countries they considered more democratic and to downgrade relations with those considered less so, Moscow actively cast itself as the protector of the more authoritarian governments against real or imagined popular threats and western encroachment. A serious casualty of this dynamic was the near collapse in 2005 of Western relations with Uzbekistan, which was and is at the geostrategic heart of Central Asia. Over time, the dynamic also led to a deterioration of ties with Azerbaijan, geostrategically the key country in the South Caucasus.

Moreover, the deteriorating situation in Afghanistan combined with the troubled U.S. invasion of Iraq to diminish the amount of human and financial resources, as well as political attention, devoted to this region. The U.S. subordinated nearly all earlier priorities in Central Asia and the Caucasus to the destruction of al Qaeda and the Taliban in Afghanistan, to fostering development in that country, and to preventing the Afghan conflict from spilling over into Central Asia. Once the government of Hamid Karzai was installed in Kabul, the annual total of USAID assistance to Afghanistan was nearly five times greater than for all five of the former Soviet states of Central Asia combined. This also led policy-makers increasingly to lose sight of the *intrinsic* value of the Caucasus and Central Asia, and to view the region principally as a conduit to Afghanistan. These two latter trends were to accelerate in the third period.

2008 and Onward: Disarray or Losing Interest?

The year 2008 marked a turning point because of two momentous events occurring within weeks of each other: in August, the Russian invasion of Georgia; and in October, the financial meltdown that shook the entire world economy. Both events had profound implications for Central Asia and the Caucasus that only gradually became clear. The Russian-Georgian war showed the West that Russia was ready and able to advance its interests through means extending far beyond mere diplomacy. Putin's Georgian war also altered regional perceptions of the West, and of America in particular. What bothered leaders in many regional capitals was not that Washington failed to defend Georgia militarily (which no one expected) but that America and Europe failed to deter Russia from an act of blatant aggression against the West's leading partner in the region, and that they subsequently failed to impose a tangible cost on Moscow for doing so. Indeed, President Obama's "reset" with Moscow, coming only months after the Georgian War, seemed to many as a reward to Moscow for bad behavior. As a result, countries everywhere in the region re-calibrated their approach to both Russia and the West.

As the economic crisis of 2008 deepened, U.S. and European leaders were preoccupied with efforts to save their own economies and deal with the social and political fallout of the financial crisis. This led to a decline in American and European attention to world events in general and to the Caucasus and Central Asia in particular. This was particularly pronounced in the case of the United States, after it launched its ill-fated "reset" with Russia, which Moscow perceived as an unspoken assertion by President Obama that problems in the relationship between Washington and Moscow were not intrinsic but had been the fault of the Bush administration. The few new American initiatives in the region either failed, like the Turkish-Armenian gambit or, like Secretary of State Clinton's New Silk Road initiative, petered out through lack of attention and support from the White House. America's inaction nourished Russia's assertiveness, which found its strongest expression in Putin's Eurasian Economic Union project. That assertiveness, however, was also born out of Russia's felt need to forestall other powers' encroachments on the region. This concern eventually focused on China, which adopted a much more assertive diplomatic posture in the region with the creation of its Silk Road Economic belt centering on Central Asia, and also the on the EU, which had launched an Eastern Partnership that included the South Caucasus. Both initiatives can best be understood as carrots that Moscow could not match; together, they forced Russia to rely heavily on sticks, as became clear in Ukraine in 2013.

Russian actions, combined with the impact of events in the Middle East, Turkey and Iran, rendered regional politics in Central Asia and the Caucasus increasingly volatile. Yet precisely at this time America was becoming ever less relevant to key regional issues. Washington no longer engaged significantly in energy diplomacy, neglected its role in conflict resolution and, following the draw-down in Afghanistan, took less notice of the region's role as a key corridor of transport and trade connecting Europe and Asia. Within Washington, the democracy and human rights lobby captured the agenda-setting power over the region. The resulting wave of "naming and shaming" caused America's ties everywhere to wither, with the near-collapse of U.S.-Azerbaijan relations in 2012-15 being only the most conspicuous and egregious example of this process. By 2015 some American policy makers were coming to acknowledge the consequences of their recent steps and missteps. In that year they launched an effort to repair relations with Azerbaijan, and a year later launched the Central Asia 5+1 format of consultations with regional states. This ended the period in which the U.S. was the only major power lacking such an institutional format for regional relations.

SOVEREIGNTY AND SECURITY

In retrospect, U.S. and EU recognition of the independence of the states of Central Asia in 1991 may seem to have been inevitable. But the experience of 1918 suggests otherwise. Armenia, Azerbaijan and Georgia had all declared their independence and were working to gain international recognition. Yet Western powers had little interest in areas they still considered to be part of Russia. Western leaders politely welcomed delegations from all three countries but support for their independence was not forthcoming. By 1991 the world had changed. Decolonization had brought recognition to many new countries in Asia and Africa. Whether or not it was inevitable that the West would recognize the new states, it became unavoidable due to a curious feature of the Soviet system itself. To avoid being tarred with the charge of recreating an "empire," Lenin and his followers defined the USSR as a federal state with nominally sovereign republics. Because of this, it was only natural that upon its dissolution its constituent members would gain membership in the United Nations. This in turn made them sovereign states under international law and would have forced the West to recognize them, even had it not wished to do so. What is surprising, then, is not the recognition itself but the vigor with which the Western powers then worked after 1991 to infuse those sovereignties with the attributes of statehood.

Even as this activity proceeded, the West was torn by disagreements over the relationship between their support for the new Russia and for the newly independent states that had arisen with the collapse of the USSR. One side argued that policy toward the former Soviet Union should be based on a Russia-first approach that would subordinate relations with the non-Russian states to the relationship with Russia. After all, proponents of this view argued, the West has a much bigger stake in Russia's future trajectory than in these smaller states; if this means allowing Russia a free hand in its former possessions, that would be an acceptable price to pay, and might even avoid unnecessary entanglements in these areas. On the other side of the debate were those who argued that the West has distinct and significant interests in the non-Russian republics. Therefore, relations with all former Soviet states should be on an equal footing, and Western states should not link their interests in, or policies toward, other republics with their relations with Russia. Indeed, supporters of this line argued that a Russia-first policy would be counter-productive even with respect to Russia, for it would encourage the worst imperial tendencies in Russian politics, while diverting attention from the urgently needed domestic reforms in that country.

In one form or another this debate has now continued for a quarter century. The Clinton Administration's first term was widely considered to have had a Russia-first slant, and the second oriented more toward an independent focus on the region. Similarly, the Bush administration sought to mend ties with Russia. But while Washington cooperated with Moscow following 9/11, it did not allow that cooperation to deter it from deepening bilateral ties with countries in Central Asia and the Caucasus that American defense planners considered equally if not more central to the war effort. The Obama Administration explicitly claimed that the "reset" would not compromise its relations with non-Russian republics. Yet many critics argued that in practice the preoccupation with Russia had a negative impact on Washington's approach to the region, for it turned out to be less a "Russia-first" policy than a "Russia-only" strategy.[1] Only with Russia's annexation of Crimea did America and Europe begin to regain their earlier focus on the sovereignty and security of the countries of the Caucasus and Central Asia.

In spite of these variations, the United States has stuck to its strategy of supporting the sovereignty and independence of these states, the divergences over time having to do with the seriousness and determination with which it has sought to advance this goal. Washington moved quickly to recognize the independence of the "successor states," to establish diplomatic relations with them, and to open embassies everywhere. This led to a broad engagement by various functional departments of the U.S. Government. Aside from development assistance, the departments of Defense, Energy, Commerce and Treasury all established deep ties with these countries.

The recognition of the regional states followed on President George H. W. Bush's proclamation of a Europe "Whole and Free," which was enshrined in the 1990 Paris Charter for a New Europe. This expressed strong support for the sovereignty and territorial integrity of all states, and for their being able to choose freely their foreign policy orientation and foreign alliances. Few signatories of the Charter had Central Asia and the Caucasus in mind, but the principles on which the new relations between former enemies would develop allowed leaders of Central Asia and the Caucasus to work vigorously in behalf of their own sovereignty, knowing that the West backed their efforts.

America's diplomatic engagement was important in elevating the international standing of the newly independent states. Aside from establishing embassies, U.S. diplomacy was instrumental in the creation of international mechanisms in which these states formed integral parts. This included the 1994 transformation of the Council for Security and Cooperation in Europe (CSCE) into a full-fledged organization and the primary forum for the management of security issues in Europe and Eurasia.

With the end of the Cold War it was significant that America did not retreat to the comfort of its own hemisphere or disengage from European affairs. On the contrary, it took a leading role in designing the structures of post-Cold War Europe. Nor was this a partisan affair: The incoming Clinton administration continued the policies initiated by the Bush administration with considerable bipartisan support in Congress. Similarly, European leaders saw the historic opportunity to build a continent 'whole and free', and embarked on a risky but ultimately highly successful enlargement of the European Union. Jointly, America and Europe enlarged NATO. These steps made central and eastern Europe enormously more prosperous and safe. Indeed, to a considerable extent this process deserves credit not only for the development of representative institutions, but also for the absence of serious strife between or within countries that joined the European family of nations.

Speaking in 1997, Deputy Secretary of State Strobe Talbott termed conflict resolution the "number one job" of the United States for the promotion of stability and security and a prerequisite for economic and democratic development. In this spirit the U.S. in 1997 assumed the co-chairmanship of the OSCE Minsk Group for resolving the Armenia-Azerbaijan conflict. This led to a flurry of activity, culminating in a strong U.S. push for a peaceful resolution of that conflict in the fall of 1999, which was aborted after the Armenian Prime Minister and Speaker of Parliament were killed by a lone attacker during a session of the Armenian parliament only hours after Talbott had left the country. Even after this setback the George W. Bush administration arranged a summit in Key West in April 2001 that once again tried and failed to resolve the conflict. France picked up the ball afterwards, and convened the Rambouillet talks in 2006 under the leadership of President Chirac, which similarly failed to arrive at a solution. These efforts did not succeed, but it was not for lack of trying. Similarly, in Tajikistan, the U.S. actively supported the UN-led negotiations that brought about an end to the civil war in 1997.

Defense relations between the newly independent states and the West have also been close, though there are considerable variations among the regional states. The U.S. Defense Department quickly sent military attachés to each Embassy and established military-to-military relationships with the newly created Ministries of Defense. The resulting programs included training and assistance to enable the new forces to throw off their Soviet past. Such initiatives were carried out bilaterally and through NATO's Partnership for Peace. This important program was created in 1994 to provide NATO with an instrument to guide its relations with all the new regional states. In the early years, American security involvement was particularly visible in Kazakhstan, on account of the nuclear weapons stationed in that country's territory, but joint programs quickly arose elsewhere, the sole exception being Turkmenistan, which had declared itself a neutral state.

The U.S.'s first major initiative in the security sphere was for the Secretary of State to work with Kazakhstan to remove nuclear weapons and fissionable material from its territory. This provided a strong tie that has remained an important building block of U.S.-Kazakhstan relations. In 1997 the U.S. military carried out its longest-distance airborne operation in history, when a first joint exercise with Central Asian militaries took place in Uzbekistan.[2] Following 9/11, the U.S. built on these relations to establish supply bases in Uzbekistan and Kyrgyzstan, which were to prove crucial to the war effort in Afghanistan.

The attention of U.S. defense planners was not limited to Central Asia. In 2001-02 Georgia came under heightened Russian pressure over the presence of Chechen fighters in its northern Pankisi Gorge, with Moscow attempting to use America's intervention in Afghanistan and the Bush Doctrine of pre-emptive strikes as precedents to build a case for intervention in Georgia.[3] But the U.S. promptly countered by launching a $64 million Train-and-Equip Program for the Georgian armed forces in February 2002. This helped Georgia to address the anarchy in the Pankisi Gorge and undermined Russia's case for intervention.[4] These developments were momentous enough to lead Russian leaders to accept, at least rhetorically, "every country's right to act to protect its security," and for Russian commentators to wonder aloud whether Russia's sphere of influence in the former Soviet

Union was a thing of the past.[5]

As regional countries developed closer ties with NATO, new governments in Georgia and Ukraine vocally sought NATO membership. In 2008 the Bush administration belatedly endorsed a path to membership for both countries, but this was rejected by European NATO members at the Bucharest summit in April. That summit came on the heels of the U.S.-led recognition of Kosovo's independence. These events prompted Moscow to launch the invasion of Georgia in August 2008. As noted above, the region is still dealing with the fallout from this invasion, which reshaped local perceptions of both the U.S. and Russia.

Russia's war aims in Georgia went beyond asserting full control over the two breakaway regions that it already dominated prior to the invasion. The aim, as expressed during the war by Russian Foreign Minister Sergey Lavrov to U.S. Secretary of State Condoleezza Rice, was regime change in Tbilisi.[6] That gambit failed for a combination of reasons. While the Georgians' staunch resistance was one important factor, another was the swift diplomacy of French President Nicolas Sarkozy, who managed to achieve a cease-fire – one detrimental to Georgian interests, to be sure, but nevertheless a cease-fire – that halted the Russian advance. And another factor was the belated but growing U.S. reaction to the war, including the U.S. repatriation of Georgian units fighting in Iraq during the war in the face of Moscow's warning that Georgia's airspace, which Russia now controlled, was not safe for U.S. aircraft. Following the war, both the U.S. and EU pledged several billion dollars in support to Georgia, which prevented the collapse of the Georgian state and enabled Georgia to continue functioning as an independent and pro-western country. The EU also launched a Monitoring Mission along the cease-fire lines in Abkhazia and South Ossetia, which deterred further Russian military adventurism.

Thus, the U.S., and to a lesser degree Europe, over the past twenty-five years have invested considerable resources in the sovereignty and security of the states of Central Asia and the Caucasus. They have done so both directly and indirectly. While we have focused here on the direct support, indirect support has been equally important, particularly in the economic realm, where Western countries combined efforts to build the major oil and gas export infrastructure that provides the backbone of the economic independence of the region.

Any discussion of Western support for security and sovereignty must also recognize the limitations and failures of these policies. Most obviously, Western commitments did not extend to providing functioning forms of collective security for the countries of the region. As Russian assertiveness increased, this created a highly volatile security situation for all the regional countries, and especially those to the West of the Caspian that refused to accept a Russian security umbrella, as Armenia and Belarus had done. Indeed, the West stood by passively as Russia created its Common Security Treaty Organization and recruited many of the regional states as members. In this sense, the West failed to build a Europe truly "whole and free." It must also be recognized that Western commitment failed to match the growing challenges to sovereignty and security in the region. Indeed, the U.S., as it became embroiled in the wars in Afghanistan and Iraq, came to view the region mainly through the prism of its Afghanistan policy rather than as a place where the U.S. had long-term interests in their own right. As a result, Washington failed to arrest the decline of relations with Uzbekistan in 2005 and subsequently in Kyrgyzstan, which led to the end of the U.S. military presence in both countries and a sharp decline in U.S. influence.

In addition, both the U.S. and EU cut the link across the Caspian in the late 2000s – the U.S. moving Central Asia to the State Department's newly created Bureau of South and Central Asian affairs, while leaving the Caucasus in the large European Bureau. The EU, more forcefully, included the Caucasus in its Eastern Partnership, but created no similar instrument for Central Asian states. These decisions had their logic, and did emphasize the European identity of the South Caucasus states. Yet the detrimental effect on Trans-Caspian communications and transportation was never accounted for; moreover, in retrospect, the organizational decisions acquired a life of their own, and also cut the conceptual strategic linkage between the Caucasus and Central Asia in the minds of Western officials and observers.

Both America and Europe also failed to grasp the importance of conflict resolution. Their actual practice grew far removed from Strobe Talbott's exhortation to make it "job one." For years following the Key West summit, America did not take seriously its role in the Minsk Group, and this neglect contributed to the escalation of conflict after 2008. Nor did America and Europe play a serious role in Georgia's conflicts until it was too late – after the 2008 war, when Russia had created a new reality on the ground. Western powers also allowed a growing disparity to arise between the commitment to territorial integrity they voiced in various conflicts, with strong support for Moldova and Ukraine, but much less support in the case of Nagorno-Karabakh.[7] In Georgia the US added insult to injury by discontinuing arms sales to Georgia after 2008. This had the blatant effect of punishing the victim of aggression, which was compounded by announcing a "reset" with Russia only months later.

Acknowledging all this, any fair-minded evaluation of Western relations with Central Asia and the Caucasus must acknowledge that serious efforts were made to shore up the sovereignty and security of these new states, even though these efforts sometimes fell short of their aim.

DEVELOPMENT OF INFRASTRUCTURES FOR THE TRANSPORT OF ENERGY AND GOODS

The development of the Caspian oil and gas resources was arguably the most significant single accomplishment of the United States and Europe in the region in the past two decades. This was strategically crucial because the inherited infrastructure, now dilapidated, had connections only to Russia, which crippled the economic sovereignty and financial viability of the new states. Without a fundamental change, Russia's monopoly over the transportation of the region's oil and gas to markets would have crippled the new sovereignties and forced them to develop under a form of neo-colonialism that would have allowed Moscow to exercise a veto power over all their strategic decisions.

The magnitude of the challenge is best illustrated by the fact that as it was being constructed, the Baku-Tbilisi-Ceyhan pipeline was the largest infrastructural project in the world. It was, first and foremost, an initiative of the local leaders – Presidents Heydar Aliyev, Eduard Shevardnadze, and Süleyman Demirel – who found common ground and guided the project to fruition together with BP and its partners. Yet the direct engagement of the United States at the highest level was crucial, for it made the new transportation infrastructure possible. But even more important, it was the question of Caspian oil that led to the development of a focused and coordinated U.S. Government strategy for the region.

Indeed, U.S. companies with a stake in the Caspian had long lobbied for greater U.S. involvement in support of their investment. By early 1995, the National Security Council's "Deputies Committee", which comprises the deputies to senior members of the Cabinet, created an inter-agency group on Caspian issues, which developed a set of U.S. priorities in the region. At the top of the list was the strengthening of the sovereignty of the countries of Central Asia and the Caucasus and the promotion of their westward orientation. Other priorities included excluding Iran from the region's energy sector and supporting American corporate interests in the region.[8]

This inter-agency group was to prove of decisive importance, for it formulated policy priorities and ensured that different branches of the U.S. Government worked in unison to promote them. These included, in addition to the State Department and NSC, the departments of Defense,

Commerce, and Energy. The inter-agency group also made possible U.S. involvement at the highest level. For example, President Clinton personally intervened to support a western pipeline route through the Caucasus. He sent a hand-delivered letter to Azerbaijani President Aliyev in September 1995, followed it up with a phone call, and invited Aliyev to Washington in 1997.[9] Clinton would attend several signing ceremonies for the Baku-Tbilisi-Ceyhan pipeline project.

The "Eurasia Transportation Corridor" designed by the Clinton administration had three components. The BTC pipeline was the most high-profile of the three, but the strategy also supported the CPC pipeline connecting Kazakhstan's immense Tengiz field with Novorossiisk on the Russian Black Sea coast; and a Trans-Caspian pipeline from Turkmenistan to Azerbaijan (which has yet to be built). The fact that the U.S. promoted the CPC project through Russia clearly indicated that the U.S. policy was not anti-Russian, but anti-monopolistic, and was focused primarily on supporting the sovereignty of the regional states.

The importance of this pipeline diplomacy is hard to overstate. It sent a clear message to regional leaders that the U.S. was invested in their sovereignty and development, and generated a common goal towards which the U.S. and regional states could work together. This in turn generated a readiness on the part of regional states to discuss and manage other more difficult elements in the relationship, such as issues of governance and human rights. In practice, U.S. diplomacy was essential in enabling Azerbaijan, Georgia, and Kazakhstan in particular, but by extension the entire region, to strengthen their statehood. In Washington this initiative was solidly bipartisan: the George W. Bush administration took over seamlessly in implementing the project, and it had considerable congressional support on both sides of the aisle.

By breaking the Russian monopoly over the transport of energy, the U.S. also facilitated China's move into Central Asia, where it would accomplish similar goals with the creation of the Turkmenistan-China pipeline system. This project, initiated by Turkmenistan in the face of considerable Chinese skepticism, has had a similar impact as the BTC pipeline.

U.S. engagement in the region's energy sector dwindled following the completion of the BTC pipeline project. Many considered Caspian energy a "done deal" which required no further attention from Washington. It was certainly not a priority of the Obama Administration, which abolished the position of special adviser on the region's energy affairs. But in reality it was not a done deal, as the giant resources of the eastern

Caspian have yet to find their way to world markets. The Central Asian states continue to view a western pipeline infrastructure, and especially a trans-Caspian pipeline, as a crucial element of diversification – this time away from a dependency on China more than Russia.

A series of further projects have had as their purpose the opening of "windows" for the export of Central Asia's hydroelectric power to Afghanistan and Pakistan and its gas to Pakistan and India, all via Afghanistan. The biggest and most consequential of these is the trans-Afghanistan pipeline project that will export Turkmen gas to Pakistan and India via Afghanistan. The U.S. tried over two decades to advance this project. But when it failed to effect an agreement between Chevron or ExxonMobil and Turkmenistan it abandoned the field. The Turkmenistan-Afghanistan-Pakistan-India pipeline (TAPI) will in all likelihood be built, but without strong U.S. or western involvement, notwithstanding its huge potential impact on the U.S.'s huge strategic investment in Afghanistan. A second major project, CASA-1000, which will send Kyrgyz and Tajik electrical energy to Pakistan via Afghanistan, has also been encouraged by the U.S. but nearly all the work to realize it has been done by the World Bank.

In 2012 in the Indian city of Chennai, Secretary of State Clinton announced the US's "New Silk Road" strategy, intended to open transport routes for both goods and energy to Pakistan and India via Afghanistan. As proposed by several papers and a book issued by the Central Asia-Caucasus Institute in Washington, it was intended that America's New Silk Road would also connect Afghanistan and Central Asia to the West, via the Caspian and Caucasus. However, this crucial dimension was dropped, whether because the drafters forgot to include it or because it would have required coordination between two separate divisions of the State Department, its Central and South Asia Bureau and its Bureau of European Affairs – always a nearly impossible task. This caused the "New Silk Road" strategy to be flawed from the outset.

Further hampering the effective implementation of what was announced as a cornerstone project was inexperienced leadership in State, grossly inadequate funding, and the failure of both the Obama White House and National Security Council to lend it public support. Suffice it to note that President Obama did not once publicly endorse his State Department's key initiative for the region. China watched this with interest and in due course appropriated the name and announced its own highly elaborated New Silk Road Economic Belt initiative.

Thus, while Washington continued to support transport projects after the completion of the BTC Pipeline, both its level of engagement and its effectiveness paled in comparison to the activity it displayed in the late 1990s and early 2000s.

EDUCATION

Education is barely mentioned in the Freedom Support Act but has long been a focus of Western initiatives in at least two ways: the support for the development of educational institutions in Central Asia and the Caucasus; and the sponsorship of programs bringing students from the region to American and European universities.

OPIC has provided considerable attention to educational facilities. It was OPIC, for example, that provided $6 million to the private American University of Central Asia to enable it to build a new and eco-friendly main building in Bishkek, and it was OPIC that extended $30 million of financing to the University of Central Asia, founded by the Aga Khan and the presidents of Kazakhstan, Kyrgyzstan, and Tajikistan. Also, private initiatives have played a major role in supporting educational innovation. American philanthropist George Soros's contribution to founding the American University of Central Asia in Bishkek, and the close involvement of many Americans and Europeans in planning the Nazarbayev University in Astana, ADA University in Baku, and University of Central Asia in Khorog, Tajikistan, Naryn, Kyrgyzstan, and Tekeli, Kazakhstan, all attest to the West's powerful impact on education in all countries of the region. OPIC has also lent support to the Georgian-American University and the University of Georgia in the Caucasus. Indeed, the rapid growth of such English language-based educational programs in every country of the Caucasus and Central Asia reflects the diversification of information sources that was beginning everywhere.

Parallel with this, EU members have promoted the establishment of both private and for-profit universities across the region, including Westminster University in Uzbekistan and a new British-based technical university in Kazakhstan. Several countries of the region participate in the EU's Erasmus program, and have adopted EU or American standards for accrediting institutions of higher education. Germany and Switzerland have collaborated with Uzbekistan and other countries to advance the long-neglected sphere of vocational-technical training across the region. Fellowships made available through the American Fulbright Program, Edmund S. Muskie Fellowship Program and dozens of other public and private programs in Europe and America directed towards high school and university students have introduced thousands of students from the Caucasus and Central Asia to western life and values.

Democracy Promotion

A prominent component of the Freedom Support Act was aid for what it called "Democracy Promotion." Among the areas of U.S. involvement, it has been the one where the least amount of success has been achieved. A glance at any international comparative index of political freedoms makes this clear; democratic progress in this region has been feeble to negative. In fairness, this is largely unrelated to U.S. policies, and more linked to the growing authoritarianism of all countries surrounding the region, as well as to internal factors in the various countries. Yet it is notable that U.S. and European democracy promotion efforts, with one exception, have been largely a failure. That exception is not Kyrgyzstan, which transitioned to a parliamentary system of government in 2010-11 largely as a result of its own internal experience. The exception is Georgia, where the reforms that followed the Rose Revolution were strongly supported by Western aid agencies and, at the political level, by their governments. But as will be seen, the main success of the Rose Revolution was in the development of governance and institutions, issues relatively low on the U.S. agenda, but higher on the agenda of European entities including the EU and Council of Europe.

Indeed, at the drafting of the Freedom Support Act, the specific contents of this broad category seemed so obvious to the drafters that they failed to specify the kinds of programs they envisioned. Nor did they provide for the support of staffs adequate to analyze the specific needs of each country, let alone to implement workable programs. As a result, much of the work in this highly sensitive sphere was outsourced to non-governmental and independent bodies.

Non-Governmental Activism

Over the years, USAID gathered a highly skilled staff of specialists in many fields, capable of carrying out the most complex and demanding projects. Nonetheless, the sheer scale of its activities made it desirable to farm out certain projects, and whole categories of projects, to independent agencies. These arrangements are codified in the form of contracts that are subject to the normal legal enforcements. Among the most visible of the many score agencies involved are the congressionally established National Democratic Institute and International Republican Institute. Beginning in 1993, these organizations have carried out worthy projects in Central Asia and the Caucasus focusing on the organization of political parties, the establishment of fair electoral processes, and the functioning of parliamentary bodies.[10] Even though the effectiveness of all these depend ultimately on the willingness and competence of the government to allow and foster electoral systems and democratic institutions, the activities of these two Institutes characteristically focus more on workshops and training programs for independent groups than on governmental agencies. There are exceptions, of course, among them projects involving the various national electoral commissions.

As the NDI and IRI expanded the number of their training programs, the possibility for misunderstanding with the governments rose. As early as 1993, both were involved with programs to train youths to participate as democratic citizens. Intelligently designed and executed by competent professionals, these programs inevitably aroused concern among some officials of newly established governments that were by no means confident in their country's ability to survive. Although the NDI and IRI programs were respectfully received even in Turkmenistan and Uzbekistan, the governments in both countries soon made it clear that their main concern was to curtail centrifugal forces in their societies and not to establish democratic institutions. Had either Institute acknowledged the governments' concerns in this area and devised ways of weaving it into the democratic narrative, it might have succeeded. They did not do this, though, and as a result the programs launched in 1993-4 were not renewed.[11]

A value of the NDI and IRI is that they both maintain research staffs that from time to time issue useful studies and opinion surveys. These, along with other studies they commission from outside analysts, are a valuable resource for all interested persons, a resource that would be rendered yet more valuable if they were issued also in local languages. Critics sometimes point out that these studies reflect their authors' or sponsors' political biases, but for the most part these are consistent with the agencies' openly announced principles.

The International Foundation for Electoral Systems (IFES) merits particular commendation not only for the quality of its research products but for the practical value of its work with local agencies and parties throughout the Caucasus and Central Asia. A fully independent non-profit organization, IFES works with governmental and private nonprofit donors, as well as with bilateral and multilateral funders. Among its funding partners are USAID, the U.S. Department of State, the United Kingdom Department for International Development, and the Canadian Department of Foreign Affairs.

In contrast to the State Department's congressionally mandated reports on democratization, which focus mainly on lapses and problems in each nation's performance and which are often characterized as "naming and shaming," IFES reports note progress as well. Thus, a study by a senior program manager at IFES on Kazakhstan's parliament points out many shortcomings in its electoral processes and functioning but at the same time acknowledges what the author considers steady progress towards a functioning party system and parliamentary body.[12] In the same vein, it is well known that money plays a major role in the politics of Georgia and, as elsewhere as well, casts a pall over the legitimacy of many elections there. IFES, working with local partners, has devoted much attention to this issue, and in the process has devised many measures that have had a positive impact there and are relevant elsewhere. IFES has also focused on civic education[13] and on the regulatory frameworks that underlie governmental funding of electoral systems, and has proposed solutions for the state-funding of political parties in Muslim-majority societies. Even in Uzbekistan it was making steady if slow progress down to the Andijan crisis in 2005, with its work with the Central Election Commission and the two education ministries. Indeed, IFES concluded that "working with the government on the promotion of change is both in IFES' interest and inevitable" if the program is truly to have a large impact.[14] The distinction between working *on* the governments of the region to foster democratic development and working *with* them is an important one, and will be examined in detail in the next chapter.

A different mode of mixed governmental and private funding for initiatives involving economic development, social betterment, and education is presented by the Eurasia Foundation. Established the U.S. Congress in 1992, the Eurasia Foundation received a Congressional endowment, which it supplements through private fundraising, grants from such private entities as the Carnegie Corporation, and contracts with various European governments. In 2003, it founded the Caucasus Research Resource Centers in Armenia, Azerbaijan, and Georgia, and in 2005 established a separate Eurasia Foundation of Central Asia. In addition to small lending programs for entrepreneurs and other initiatives in the sphere of economics education, EF has facilitated the establishment of private publishers in several countries, journalism outlets, and public opinion research groups. In all three of these areas EF support has been nearly unique, and of great value.

Purely private foundations have also made significant contributions to the political empowerment of citizens of post-Soviet states, economic development, and innovations in education. Among the many foundations that have played active roles are the Soros Foundation, which has funded activities in the realm of human rights, journalism, and education; the Carnegie Corporation, whose support for locally-based analytic work has been mentioned; the Aga Khan Foundation, which has supported projects in Tajikistan and Kyrgyzstan to promote economic and social development and founded the University of Central Asia; the MacArthur Foundation, which gave a number of grants to support study in the region during the 1990s; and Human Rights Watch and Freedom House. Several of these, notably the Aga Khan Foundation, have benefited from lucrative support from USAID and other international organizations, but all are based on private endowments as well. In Armenia, a large number of Diaspora Armenian organizations have provided significant private funding in every area.

Supplementing these sources are a number of individual European governments. Especially notable among them is Switzerland, which established programs in the South Caucasus in 1988, and in Kyrgyzstan in 1993. It continues its active support for economic and social development and water and energy management down to the present, but has focused increasingly on Tajikistan. Finland has also provided steady project support, which is unique in its recognition of the importance of national banks to economic progress. Sweden was active in the entire region down to the first decade of the new century, but withdrew from Central Asia thereafter, while remaining one of the largest donors to Georgia. Moreover, together with Poland, Sweden took the initiative with the creation of the Eastern Partnership in 2009. Canada also withdrew from Central Asia; its International Center for Human Rights and Democratic Development functioned to 2012, when it was closed. The United Kingdom's Department for International Development is one of the largest donors in the region, having spent upwards of $15 million yearly, mainly in Kyrgyzstan and Tajikistan.

Westminster Foundation for Democracy announced a broad program but has been unable to sustain it on an annual budget of only $5 million, while the European Endowment for Democracy, established in 2012, commanded a budget of only $11 million by 2015. Germany, the Netherlands, and the Baltic states have also lent support for projects in Central Asia and the Caucasus, with Latvia focusing its presidency of the European Union on Central Asian issues. Japan also moved quickly after 1993 to lend support to disaster relief (mud slides, flooding, etc.) in Central Asia but diminished its involvement down to 2015, when it renewed its engagement with the region.

Shifting Priorities in Western Development Assistance

Revising Strategies: the U.S.

U.S. development assistance to Central Asia and the Caucasus has gone through numerous shifts. The earliest period following independence saw a priority given to humanitarian assistance, which shifted to long-term development assistance as immediate crises were addressed. Yet given the time needed for development specialists to identify priorities, devise and implement programs, the financial shifts triggered by 9/11 – and subsequently the Iraq war - came fairly rapidly following their establishment in Central Asia and the Caucasus. As such, the U.S. focused on fostering development in Afghanistan, and on preventing the Afghan conflict from spilling over into Central Asia. Not only was the annual total of USAID assistance to Afghanistan soon several times greater than for all eight former Soviet states combined, but skilled personnel were shifted to south of the Amu Darya in order to hasten the creation of new institutions, a viable economy, and a more open state in Afghanistan. To this day Afghanistan far surpasses the countries of Central Asia and the Caucasus combined in the number of USAID projects there. The total number of projects per country for the entire period 2001 to 2016 include 20 for Kazakhstan, 28 for Kyrgyzstan, 23 for Tajikistan, 14 for Turkmenistan, and 17 for Uzbekistan. By contrast, Afghanistan could claim a total of 114, more than all the others combined.

USAID in 2014 announced what it called a new strategy for the region. It declared that "USAID now has an opportunity to adopt a more pragmatic and possibly more modest but achievable approach, acknowledging the complexities of this challenging region while retaining a commitment to deal directly and creatively with them [sic.]."[15]

Turning to USAID expenditures as a whole for the past quarter century, we must first note that the agency has yet to publish online information on projects it carried out between 1992 and 2001.[16] Expenditures by country are available, however. The graphs presented below detail the rise and fall by country. Focusing only on the five Central Asian states that were formerly part of the Soviet Union, we see a sharp rise in expenditures after 9/11, peaking in 2006 and dropping thereafter until 2011. The rise traces to fears that Taliban-type radicalism could spread northward and had to be countered through economic and institutional development. The five-year drop that followed is peculiar, because it came on the heels of Russia's invasion of another post-Soviet state, Georgia, and at the time of a revolution in Kyrgyzstan. Spending increased thereafter, however, and remained at around $120 million per annum until 2017, when USAID managed to increase its regional budget once more.

The new phase of USAID activity that was announced in 2014 was less a result of a fresh *opportunity* than of a stark *necessity*, dictated by budgetary constraints caused by the need to keep U.S. troops in Afghanistan and by the spread of terrorism in the Middle East and beyond. The new strategy, then, sought to do more with less. The document identifies four priorities:.

First, it proposed expanding U.S.-regional trade, intraregional trade, and trade with and through Afghanistan in order to strengthen that country's economy and to open for Central Asia a "window" to Pakistan, India and Southeast Asia, as envisioned in the U.S.-initiated New Silk Road Program.

The second arm of the strategy was to strengthen regional cooperation in energy and water use – both important and even urgent concerns. But USAID had been supporting activity in these areas since the 1990s. Moreover, both the European Union and the World Bank also identified water and energy as priorities during this period. This is all laudable, but posed serious problems of coordination, not to mention confusion on the Central Asians' side. Observing the multiplication of separate initiatives, it was not unreasonable for some in the region to wonder whether this U.S. strategic priority would not go the way of the many international initiatives mounted in the 1990s to "solve" the Aral Sea problem.

The third priority of the 2014 strategy was by far the most innovative and interesting, for it called for building "more effective and inclusive governance institutions that serve the public good." Here, for nearly the first time, the focus is on the responsiveness and effectiveness of governmental institutions. In other words, USAID proposed to link arms with Central Asian governments to reform those parts of their civil services that most directly affect citizens. By embracing this as a *precondition* for democracy, USAID tacitly acknowledged that previous attempts to "build democracy" were like a builder who wants to construct the second floor of a house without first building the basement. Given the venal, ineffective, and ruinous heritage of Soviet administration in these countries, this decision was positive indeed, even if it was slow in coming.

The fourth focus of the new strategy was on health, a positive and noncontroversial sphere where much good can be accomplished. This in turn links with a further series of "priorities" that arise from Presidential initiatives: "Feed the Future," the Global Health Initiative, Global Climate Change Initiative, and gender. None of these is subject to USAID discretion. While individually worthy, together these additional priorities run the risk of diverting attention and funds from the priority areas established by USAID itself on the basis of two decades of experience.

The Evolving Role of the European Union

The European Union must be credited for its support for economic and social development projects in both the Caucasus and Central Asia. The EU has significantly ramped up its aid programs in Central Asia, with disbursements of €675 million in 2007-13, with an indicative program for 2014-20 of over €1 billion. The EU priorities have been to boost sustainable development, promote stability and security, and build regional cooperation. Since 2009, the EU has differentiated between Central Asia and the South Caucasus, with the latter being included in the Eastern Partnership instrument, along with Ukraine and Moldova. The Eastern Partnership differs from traditional development assistance in that it provides opportunities for integration with the EU itself, by adoption of over two thirds of the Union's *acquis communautaire* for countries electing to sign Association Agreements and negotiate Deep and Comprehensive Free Trade Agreements. In the South Caucasus, only Georgia has implemented such an agreement; Armenia negotiated an agreement, but chose instead to join the Russia-led Eurasian Union. Azerbaijan has not shown interest in the DCFTA, suggesting instead a Strategic Partnership Agreement with the EU, which is under negotiation. Under the Eastern Partnership, nearly €2.5 billion was available for cooperative programs. For 2014-17 the EU has an indicative financial allocation of €335-410 million only for Georgia. Figures for Armenia and Azerbaijan are €140-170 million and €77-94 million, respectively.

A European analyst proudly claims that, in comparison to that of the U.S., "the EU's approach is much more diverse and focuses on aspects of human security, which it tries to support through projects and funding for rule of law, good governance, and water management, but at the same time supporting Central Asian border management and so on. In doing so the EU has substantially more resources at its disposal and the EU's objectives in Central Asia are also much broader than merely security and partnership. Nonetheless, it is strange that the EU and NATO do not liaise much in general, particularly when it comes to policies on, and ties with, Central Asia... U.S. and European policies towards Central Asia are increasingly divergent, the EU takes a broad approach by looking at a whole spectrum of issues, from energy interests to the promotion of democratic values and human rights to security interests, while the U.S.'s approach is becoming narrower by concentrating foremost on (hard) security matters and seeing Central Asia primarily through an Afghanistan lens."[17]

To the extent that these claims are based on post-9/11 activities, they are at least partially valid. The EU did indeed increase funding for activities in the "soft" areas enumerated in the statement. Before then, however, it was the U.S. that played the lead role, a role that continued after 9/11, albeit with diminished resources. It should also be noted that the EU's focus on soft power must be tempered by the fact that by its very nature the EU is unable to address hard security issues. To be sure, the new framework for EU-Central Asian relations introduced a decade later includes consultation and activity in the sphere of security. But the EU's own founding documents severely limit such engagement to such minor issues as border management and long prevented the EU from touching on the larger security issues that are the most urgent concern of the states of Central Asia themselves.

In the Caucasus, the EU was compelled to take action in the aftermath of the Russian invasion of Georgia. Since 2008, it has implemented the EU Monitoring Mission along the administrative boundary lines separating Georgia from Abkhazia and South Ossetia. While the cease-fire agreement that ended the violence provided for an international presence in those territories as well, Russia continues to refuse to let in the EUMM in what it now considers "independent states". That said, the EUMM plays a crucial role in monitoring developments along the frontlines, and is thus able authoritatively to refute recurrent Russian accusations of Georgian violations of the cease-fire, while at least registering and documenting Russian violations. At the same time, the unarmed mission is unable to do anything to prevent it. As for the Armenia-Azerbaijan conflict, the EU has adopted the position that it would gladly participate in a post-conflict resolution mission, and potentially disburse large sums toward it. However, the EU has studiously refused to get more seriously engaged in making such a resolution possible.[18]

In 2007 the EU reorganized its activities in Central Asia. The European Council approved a new "Strategy for a New Partnership" with Central Asia that provided for regular dialogue on human rights, education, environment, water management, trade, and economic relations, as well as an increase in funding for these activities. While the EU's approach to some of these areas differed from U.S. governmental and private organizations, the list of subject areas is nearly identical to what USAID and other American entities had been doing for a decade.

A 2012 Progress Report[19] on the EU's work in Central Asia finally acknowledged the reality that had driven American policy towards Central Asia since 9/11 and was the cause of the increasing divergence between programs of the U.S. and EU: Afghanistan. As if declaring a new discovery, the EU's Progress Report declared that "the region faces new and growing challenges—especially in Afghanistan—and that security issues have come to the fore in relations with the EU." Then, in a formulation that appeared to equate the EU's role with NATO's serious commitment to Afghanistan's security and reconstruction for a decade, it announced that "NATO, *as well as the EU*, is concerned about the development of Afghanistan over the coming years."

Far more constructive was the EU's decision to reorganize its relations with, and assistance to, Central Asia on a *regional* basis rather than on bilateral relations, as had heretofore been the case. Naming a new Special Representative for the entire region, the EU for the first time engaged senior officials in wide-ranging discussions and programs that crossed national boundaries. In taking this positive step it emulated Japan's "Japan Plus Central Asia" structure, adding, however a regional security program as well. Even though the latter lacked, and still lacks content, it provides a useful format for regional discussions not dominated by either Russia or China. The United States was not to take a comparable step until 2015-16, and then under multi-year pressure first from Uzbekistan and then from Kazakhstan. The EU-Central Asia Monitoring (EUCAM) was established with support from the Soros Foundation in 2008 to monitor the implementation of EU programs in Central Asia and to serve as a knowledge hub for research pertaining to those fields, yet with a strong focus on a single issue area, human rights and democracy. In the same spirit, such European research entities as the Centre for European Policy Studies in Brussels carry out parallel studies on topics pertinent to EU activities in the region.

NATO

Meanwhile NATO in 2011-12 redoubled its efforts in Central Asia. Over several preceding years its main focus had been on supplying its forces in Afghanistan through the Northern Distribution Network and through bases in Central Asia, and on eliciting Central Asian support for reconstruction in Afghanistan. In both areas it had achieved success, with Kazakhstan and Uzbekistan being particularly active, the former through military support and development assistance programs and the latter by extending (with support from the Asia Development Bank) its railroad network from the Afghan border to Mazar-e-Sharif. As the NDN and massive provisioning programs were now being phased out, NATO established a new Liaison Office for Central Asia with a civilian head and staff that includes a transportation officer. Based on the new Strategic Concept adopted at the 2010 Lisbon Summit, this new arrangement emphasized shared security concerns, and advanced such fundamental principles as interoperability, defense sector reform, officer training, environmental concerns in the security sector, the safe disposal of munitions in regions bordering Afghanistan, and participation in NATO-led peacekeeping operations.

International Financial Institutions and Private Firms

Any assessment of western investment in development and assistance programs for the Caucasus and Central Asia must include both the World Bank, in which the U.S. is the main investor, the European Bank for Reconstruction and Development (EBRD), and the Asian Development Bank (ADB). Indeed, the World Bank, along with USAID, is the single largest investor in the region's development, while the EBRD has a total cumulative investment of over €15 billion in the eight countries.[20]

The World Bank (WB) distinguished itself from the outset by taking a *regional* rather than purely national approach.[21] This was evident above all in CASA-1000, its highly successful project to market Kyrgyz and Tajik hydroelectric power in Afghanistan and Pakistan, which was part of its umbrella Central Asia Energy Water Development Program (CAEWDP). Among less heralded activities under this rubric is the WB's successful effort to modernize hydrometeorological activity in the upstream countries, and to enhance regional cooperation in this important sphere. Other quite different initiatives focus on migration and remittances, on health, HIV/AIDS, and also on transport, on which WB cooperates closely with the Asian Development Bank and its regionally-based CAREC program. This ADB initiative has been of paramount importance to the support of new transport corridors in Central Asia, but its lamentable failure fully to link those corridors to both Europe and the Indian subcontinent have left a gap which China's Silk Road Economic Belt program only partially fills.

Parallel with its region-wide programs, the World Bank has engaged in bilateral projects throughout the region, with expenditures in Kyrgyzstan and Tajikistan alone surpassing $1 billion since 1992. These comprise a bewildering array of initiatives, many of which are designed to promote trade and market-based commerce and the institutional infrastructure needed to support it.

In sharp contrast to the World Bank's highly diversified portfolio of projects, the European Bank for Reconstruction and Development (EBRD) has focused single-mindedly on the transition to a market economy, a goal it has advanced in every country through a wide variety of programs that include promoting cross-border trade, improving municipal services, and empowering women entrepreneurs. It has mounted 215 projects in Kazakhstan, 198 in Georgia, 159 in Azerbaijan, 152 in Armenia, 138 in Kyrgyzstan, 103 in Tajikistan, 54 in Uzbekistan and 53 in Turkmenistan. The EBRD has concentrated its support above all on Kazakhstan. In the process of this work, it has expended $6.5 billion[22] on banking reform, modernizing agribusinesses, renewable energy, waste management, transport, and other sectors. Adding this to the $6 billion that the World Bank has spent there, it makes Kazakhstan by far the biggest recipient of international financing in both the Caucasus and Central Asia. By contrast, the EBRD's current portfolio of projects in Uzbekistan is €12 million, compared to €2.4 billion in Kazakhstan, and no new initiatives are planned there. This can be contrasted to the World Bank, which has signed a new Country Partnership Framework with Uzbekistan for 2016-2020. Supported by a fund of more than $3 billion, the Partnership is built on that country's goal of achieving upper middle-income status by 2030 by increasing the economy's competitiveness, improving the business environment, and developing its infrastructure to support rapid job creation.

The rationale for EBRD's focus is that Kazakhstan, with its energy resources and modern mentality, has the potential to become a regional driver for reform. Besides, such an approach has the virtue of developing models for success that can then find a more positive reception elsewhere.

Separate from these initiatives by public bodies and not-for-profit foundations and organizations are the countless investments by private American and European firms in both the Caucasus and Central Asia.

American and European Investments

To speak of but one country, more than 160 U.S. firms are members of the American Chamber of Commerce in Kazakhstan. Similar organizations exist in all regional states for the purpose of promoting bilateral contacts in business. One of these, the U.S.-Azerbaijan Chamber of Commerce, along with the U.S. Government, played an important role in bringing about the crucial Baku-Tbilisi-Ceyhan Pipeline project, a key bulwark of prosperity and sovereignty in the Caucasus. While American and European investments were focused initially in oil and gas and mining, they have since become increasingly diversified as a result of cooperative work with the various governments.

Both private and governmentally-owned firms from many more countries have invested in the regions. Notable among them are China, Japan, Russia, and South Korea, but countless others must be acknowledged as well, including Australia, Indonesia, and Malaysia, Singapore, Taiwan, and Turkey. But it has been the West that has assumed the lion's share of the burden of helping these new states effect a smooth transition from Communist rule and a state-dominated economy.

SUMMING UP

We have seen that the West has undergirded many vital initiatives in the economic sphere including the above-mentioned Baku-Tbilisi-Ceyhan pipeline project, the World Bank's CASA-1000 electricity export initiative, and transport projects to link the region to the South and West under the EU's Traceca, the ADB's CAREC program, and the American New Silk Road. The West has also engaged actively with the Caucasus and Central Asia in the political and diplomatic sphere. In addition to the many initiatives cited above, the U.S. and France have also figured centrally in the long but frustrating Minsk Process to defuse the Karabakh conflict between Armenia and Azerbaijan. Thanks to all this, countries in both Central Asia and the Caucasus that seek to achieve a balanced and positive relationship with their major neighbors, China and Russia, have been able to look to the West as a major and reliable factor in the economic and diplomatic balancing that is at the heart of such strategies.

In light of all this, it is no overstatement to say that no other country or grouping of countries comes close to either the U.S. or the EU, let alone the two of them together, in the amount of their assistance, the range of fields to which it has been applied, or the amount and quality of expert know-how made available to the new states of Central Asia and the Caucasus since their establishment as new sovereignties.

Appendix: USAID Expenditures in Central Asia

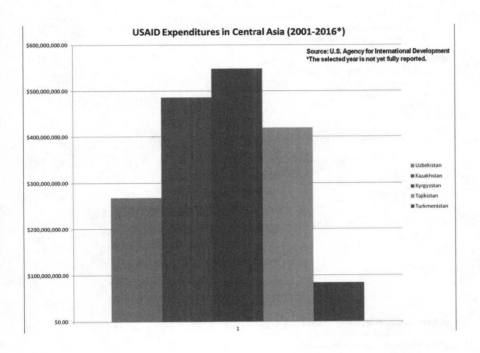

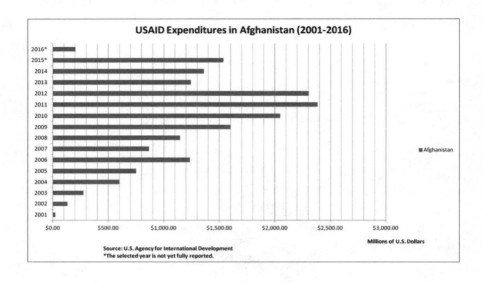

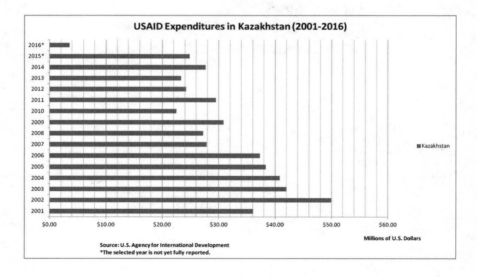

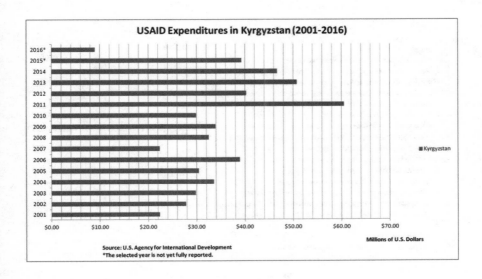

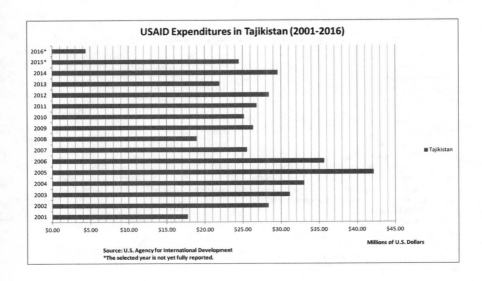

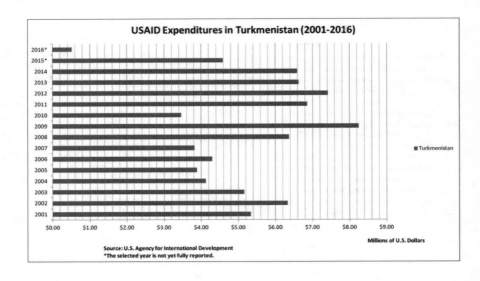

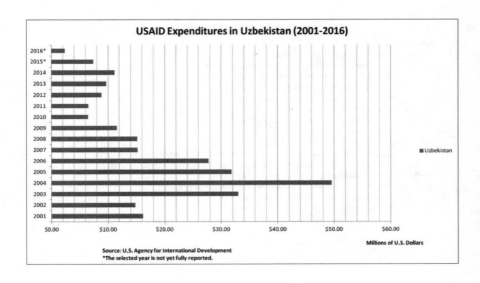

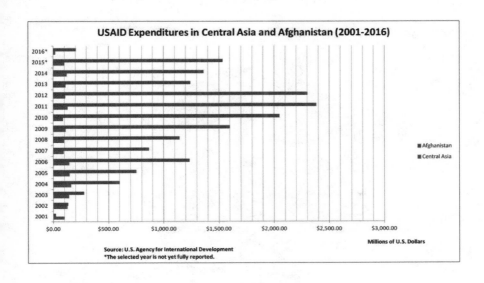

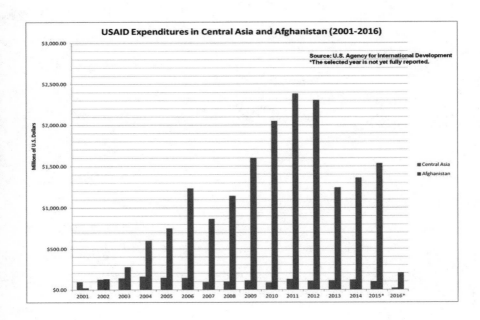

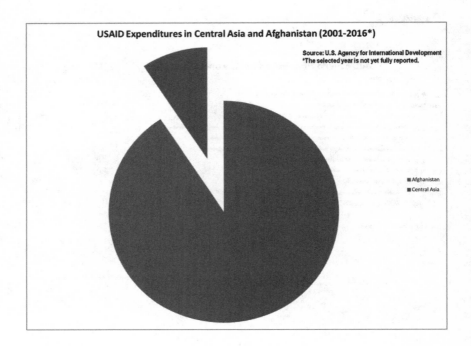

USAID Expenditures in Central Asia and Afghanistan (2001-2016*)

Source: U.S. Agency for International Development
*The selected year is not yet fully reported.

■ Afghanistan
■ Central Asia

ENDNOTES

1. David J. Kramer, "U.S. Abandoning Russia's Neighbors", *Washington Post*, May 15, 2010.
2. "Centrazbat '97 Set to Get Underway", UPI, September 14, 1997. (http://www.upi.com/Archives/1997/09/14/CENTRAZBAT-97-set-to-get-underway/2357874209600/)
3. Julie Wilhelmsen and Geir Flikke, "Evidence of Russia's Bush Doctrine in the CIS", *European Security*, vol. 14 no. 3, 2005, 387-417.
4. Rick Fawn, "Russia's Reluctant Retreat from the Caucasus", *European Security*, vol. 11 no. 4, 2002, pp. 131-150.
5. Igor Torbakov, "Does Moscow's Reaction to Developments in Georgia Herald the End of Eurasia?", *Eurasianet*, March 4, 2002. (http://www.eurasianet.org/departments/insight/articles/eav030502.shtml)
6. Condoleezza Rice, *No Higher Honor: A Memoir of My Years in Washington*, Random House, p. 688.
7. See Svante E. Cornell, ed., *The International Politics of the Armenian-Azerbaijani Conflict: The Original "Frozen" Conflict and European Security*, New York: Palgrave, 2017.
8. See S. Frederick Starr and Svante E. Cornell, eds., *The Baku-Tbilisi-Ceyhan Pipeline: Oil Window to the West*, Washington: Central Asia-Caucasus Institute & Silk Road Studies Program, 2005. (https://www.silkroadstudies.org/resources/pdf/Monographs/2005_01_MONO_Starr-Cornell_BTC-Pipeline.pdf); Jofi Joseph, "Pipeline Diplomacy: The Clinton Administration's Fight for Baku-Ceyhan", Woodrow Wilson School, Case Study 1/99, 1999.
9. Dan Morgan and David B. Ottaway, "Azerbaijan's Riches alter the Chessboard", Washington Post, October 4, 1998, p. A1.
10. The direction of future IRI activity is forecast in "IRI: First Youth Leadership and Democracy Training Workshop, Uzbekistan and Turkmenistan, 1993," IRI PM-can-510-112288.
11. National Republican Institute, "Trip Report for October and November Missions to Tashkent and Ashgabat, NRI, IRI 2, PD-ABU-546-112300.
12. Anthony Clive Bowyer, *Parliament and Political Parties in Kazakhstan*, Silk Road Paper. Central Asia Caucasus Institute, 2008.
13. Gina Gilbreath Holdar, David B. Ogle, *Evaluation of IFES Civic Education Programs in Kazakhstan, Kyrgyz Republic and Tajikistan*, Washington, 2003.
14. Anthony Bowyer et al, IFES, Republic of Uzbekistan: Final Project report: October 1, 1997-September 30, 2002, Washington, 2005.
15. U.S. Agency for International Development. https://www.usaid.gov/central-asia-regional/history; for the strategy see U.S. Agency for International Development. (2014). Central Asia: Regional Development Cooperation Strategy 2015-2019. at: http://pdf.usaid.gov/pdf_docs/pbaab464.pdf
16. All budgetary information is drawn from the website: https://www.usaid.gov/
17. Joos Boonstra, "NATO and Central Asia: the Two Elephants that Never Meet," *Eucam Watch*, No.11, February, 2012, p. 1.

18. Svante E. Cornell, "The European Union and the Armenian-Azerbaijani Conflict: Lessons Not Learned", in Cornell, *The International Politics of the Armenian-Azerbaijani Conflict*, pp. 149-172.
19. European Union External Action, https://eeas.europa.eu/central_asia/docs/20120628_progress_report_en.pdf
20. All information on EBRD activities is from its official website: http://www.ebrd.com/where-we-are.html
21. All information on WB is from its official website: http://www.world-bank.org
22. All information is from the official EBRD website: http://www.ebrd.com

A Deeper Look: Shortcomings of Western Policy

The downward spiral of the USSR during its last decade was widely reported and analyzed in the West, but its sudden collapse on 26 December, 1991, was as great a surprise to Washington and the capitals of Europe as it was to most Soviet citizens. Such words as "decline", "decay," or "evolution" gave everyone time to ponder what was occurring and to frame careful plans for the future. "Collapse" demanded immediate action.

The CIA had been conducting gaming exercises for a year, but when one of them concluded in November 1990 that the USSR could quickly collapse it was too timid to pass this prediction to the White House.[1] Washington was caught completely off guard. Yet the American government had no doubt about the importance and urgency of the moment. President George H. W. Bush declared it "the most important foreign policy opportunity of our time,"[2] and many in Congress echoed his sentiment.

But how to respond to it? The collapse itself had occurred with little violence and in near-complete silence. It had been rendered inevitable a few weeks earlier when Russian president Boris Yeltsin and the heads of the Republics of Ukraine and Belarus signed an accord effectively dissolving the Soviet Union. The final blow was announced not on the field of battle but by a press release. And yet it was, by any measure, an epochal event that called for an epochal response. The legislation which the U.S. adopted in response, the Freedom Support Act, would guide much of the American government's response.

THE FREEDOM SUPPORT ACT: WHAT BENCHMARKS FOR ASSISTANCE?

Congressman Lee Hamilton, chairman of the House Foreign Affairs Sub-Committee on Europe, had approvingly characterized the legislation that was developed as "by far the most important political vote that most members will cast in their careers in Congress." A few senators opposed it on the grounds that the money it called for should go instead to domestic needs, but it nonetheless passed the Senate by a vote of 76-20 and was unanimously approved by the House. The only strongly critical voice came from former president Richard Nixon, who attacked President Bush's plan as "a pathetically inadequate response in light of the opportunities and dangers we face in the crisis in the former Soviet Union."[3]

Even before the final vote, an element of politicization had crept into the text, when Senator John F. Kerry introduced a motion (Section 907a) banning all government-to-government support under the Act to Azerbaijan, on the grounds that it was "blockading" Armenia. Effectively promoted by the domestic Armenian lobby, which had a strong base in Kerry's home state of Massachusetts, the amendment was silent on the fact that the Armenian army in fact occupied Azerbaijani territory at the time, and would soon move on to occupy almost one sixth of that country's land.[4]

The drafting of the Freedom Support Act had been done in haste, but was greatly facilitated by the existence of a kind of ready-made model in the form of the Helsinki Final Act of 1975. This important document, signed by thirty-two nations, had been the culmination of a decade of negotiations to contain the most negative military and geopolitical tensions of the Cold War and to open new channels for commercial interaction and cultural exchange between the USSR and the West. It achieved this diplomatic slight-of-hand by breaking down the overall relationship into three sub- categories: military and political; economic; and human rights (including freedom of the press). "Slight-of-hand," because both the USSR and West were eager to find some common ground in trade, scientific, and cultural interaction, even as they knew profound differences would persist in the political and military spheres. The Freedom Support Act adopted not only the formal structure of the Helsinki Final Act but its assumptions as well.

The Freedom Support Act drew heavily on the Helsinki Final Act, and especially its division of the overall relationship into three "baskets,"[5] military, economic, and "political." However, it modified the Helsinki formula in one important respect, namely, by eliminating mention of the political relationship and by replacing it with a new "basket" labeled "democratization," so as to reflect the U.S.'s dedication to promoting that principle of government. Human rights remained part of this "basket." Most other details were transferred wholesale, including the Helsinki agreement's prohibition against the use of force to change borders and against all claims on neighbors' land. Since this was precisely the situation that prevailed in the Caucasus, where Armenia had used force to gain control of Azerbaijani territory, it would seem that Armenia, not Azerbaijan, should have been disqualified. But this did not happen. Instead, Congress approved Kerry's Section 907 banning Azerbaijan from receiving aid under the new legislation. By distorting its own legislation in order to satisfy domestic U.S. political pressures, Congress corrupted its own best intentions from the outset. It is telling that in a bipartisan fashion, all subsequent U.S. administrations opposed this unfortunate legislation but were unwilling or unable to have it repealed.

In adopting the promotion of democracy as one of its three main goals, the Act embarked on new territory. True, President Woodrow Wilson had included the promotion of democracy as one of the Fourteen Points by which he justified America's entry into World War I, a war, he said, that would "make the world safe for democracy." But in spite of Wilson's burst of democracy promotion, it did not figure prominently in U.S. diplomacy over the intervening generations down to 1992. Nor, obviously, had it figured in the Helsinki agreement. Now, in other words, the U.S. Congress launched U.S. diplomacy into new and uncharted waters. Given the collapse of Communism across the former Soviet bloc, this seemed an obvious and reasonable course. In reality it proved to be neither.

How does one promote democracy? In recent years there has grown up a valuable body of writing that seeks to identify the links between democracy, economic development, and security. In Chapter 6 we shall review some of this literature more closely. For now, let us note simply that the official bodies in both Washington and Brussels charged with implementing the "democracy agenda" tended to treat it not as the outcome of a complex series of relations and preconditions but as an independent variable. A similar assumption underlay much of the talk of market economies and the institutions that embody them. This unstated assumption had the great advantage of enabling bureaucrats to assign the promotion of "democracy" or of "market economies" to separate offices and charge them with doing the job, largely in isolation from other factors and conditions and the tasks that needed to be accomplished to advance them.

This was a time when the "transition paradigm" dominated western thinking on political evolution. As democratization scholar Thomas Carothers observed, the core assumption of this paradigm was that "any country moving *away* from dictatorial rule can be considered a country in transition *toward* democracy." Further, it assumed that underlying conditions –whether economic, political, or institutional – "will not be major factors in either the onset or the outcome of the transition process". In addition, the predominant thinking derive from developments in southern Europe and Latin America. Based on this experience, it assumed that democratic transition was "being built on coherent, functioning states". Yet as Carothers puts it, this line of thinking "did not give significant attention to the challenge of a society trying to democratize while it is grappling with the reality of building a state from scratch or coping with an existent but largely nonfunctional state."[6]

What served bureaucratic neatness and clarity did not advance the cause of democratization in practice. The reason for this is that by treating "democratization" as an independent variable, western governments and private foundations stripped away from it all the preconditions that were in fact essential to its success. Indeed, with two exceptions, there was practically no discussion of preconditions. The first—that democracy was incompatible with rule by a Communist Party—had been addressed with the collapse of the Soviet system. The second concerned the hypothesis that democracy thrives best in economically developed societies.[7] This was comfortably laid to rest by frequent citations of India's experience since independence. Armed with the confidence that a poor country can also be democratic, western policymakers conveniently ignored all social and cultural factors that might have facilitated India's success, and did not ask whether these were present in Central Asia and the Caucasus.

This, then, was the frame of mind that prevailed in the United States and Europe at the time the Freedom Support Act was drafted. None of this was seriously challenged at the time, either from within western governments or without, by competing political forces in the West or by independent analysts or scholars. The Act does not treat "democratization" as something embedded in a series of social, economic, institutional and political conditions, each of which had to be fostered before democracy could flower, but as the close relative of "human rights." Neither did European countries' bilateral assistance programs do so. However, it should be noted that the Council of Europe, for the states of the South Caucasus, did focus very strongly on institution-building; and the EU's development programs have been considerably more focused on building institutions. The EU launched a Rule of Law Mission in Georgia in 2004, the first such initiative launched under the European Security and Defense Policy. The EU Strategy for Central Asia, launched in 2007, made rule of law and good governance key themes alongside human rights and democratization, and its focus is based on agreements between the EU and regional governments. The EU terms its Rule of Law Initiative a "key element" of its strategy; and its Rule of Law Platform focuses on "Administrative Law, Economic Governance, Criminal Justice and Judicial Reform."[8]

The EU's divergent approach may be related to the fact that its large-scale activity in Central Asia began only in 2007; and that it did not follow the path dependence of other development programs. Overall, however, it is difficult to escape the conclusion that Western decision-makers – and certainly the human rights lobby – approached the task of democratization as one that could be best promoted through the same means by which the West had promoted human rights in the USSR and Eastern Europe, namely, by supporting the actions of principled individuals and groups of citizen-activists, either self-funded or with support from the outside. Had this not worked in Poland, in Czechoslovakia, and eventually in the USSR itself? Most western policymakers and experts had no doubt that they already had in hand the key to success, and that democracy would emerge if only they lent sufficient support to those non-governmental forces across the region that declared their commitment to democracy.

Many, if not most, U.S. and European programs in support of democracy and human rights were implemented by locally organized non-governmental organizations (NGOs) that were engaged through contracts with the sponsor. This approach accorded with the prevailing ideology, which held that NGOs could transform governments and societies "from below." However, governments in the region were skeptical of NGOs from the outset, seeing them as a potentially dangerous centrifugal forces and pluralism at a time when, they feared, sovereignty itself was still at stake. The fact that they received funding from abroad and not from local citizens inevitably made them suspect in the eyes not only of their critics but of many ordinary citizens. Neither the U.S. nor EU made any effort to accommodate or address this charge. Basing their approach on the experience of such organizations as Solidarity in Poland, Charter 77 and Civic Forum in Czechoslovakia, and Memorial in Russia, they blithely assumed that what worked against an entrenched but stagnant Soviet system would be equally effective against the governments of newly sovereign states that were actively struggling to preserve their very existence. With the sole possible exceptions of Georgia and Kyrgyzstan, this assumption proved false. But both Europeans and Americans clung to their assumptions, and as a result found themselves in many spheres working *on* regional governments more than *with* them, and often in fact *against* them.

It is important here to acknowledge fully the many valuable contributions that western-sponsored NGOs made to their societies during the quarter century since independence and continue to make today. In such fields as public health, women's rights, agriculture, basic education, information, and local water management they have provided invaluable assistance that could not readily have come from any other source. It is true that over time many NGOs fell prey to the corruption prevailing in their societies, and it is true that some seemed to have set themselves in clear opposition to the national governments. These were exceptions, however, to a worthy record of achievement. The problem is that all too often they paraded themselves as an alternative to governmental action rather than a supplement to it, and needlessly aroused suspicions regarding their motives and those of their foreign sponsors.

The frame of mind that informed the one-sided support for NGOs and citizen action led to a further assumption that is as important as it is unexamined, namely, that democratization would come about as a result of independent and heroic citizens of the Caucasus and Central Asia acting *on* their governments. In other words, the West operated on the assumption that democracy would come about through the workings of the very democratic processes that all acknowledged to be absent. Instead of facing directly this brute conundrum, they pointed to the success of pressure groups in Communist Eastern Europe that had worked outside and against the governments, not with them. But this conveniently ignored one absolutely crucial factor: that the governments of Poland, Czechoslovakia, the USSR and other countries of the Soviet bloc did not *evolve* into quasi-democracies under pressure from citizen activists, but *collapsed.* Only after the collapse of Communist regimes were they able to strip away at least some of the detritus of the Soviet system and begin serious discussion of what to replace it with.

The U.S. Congress, Human Rights Watch, The Soros Foundation's Open Society Institute, and other lobby groups may not have understood this, but it was utterly clear to all the newly formed governments in both Central Asia and the Caucasus. These were young governments beset by various threats to their very existence, both internal and external.

Their new leaders were acutely aware not of their autocratic power but of their appalling weakness in the face of the many problems that beset them. Whatever the framers of the Freedom Support Act may have thought (and there is no evidence that they seriously considered this), their legislation was perceived across the Caucasus and Central Asia as threatening to the very governments that had arisen after the collapse of the Communist system.

This is not surprising. The new governments faced existential threats arising both internally and externally. They were staffed by people who were new to their jobs in independent states and had nothing to guide them but their experience under the USSR. One of the new leaders—Imomali Rakhmonov in Tajikistan – faced a civil war, while another – Saparmurad Niyazov in Turkmenistan – found himself at the head of a state that was unitary only in name and otherwise tribal in character. Every one of the other states of the Caucasus and Central Asia was equally fragile, and perceived as such by their leaders – so much so that these groped for symbols that could be used to provide a sense of unity and common history for their populations. In Uzbekistan, this meant casting Tamerlane in the role as an Uzbek national hero; Kyrgyzstan found the purportedly 1,000-year old epos of Manas; Tajikistan reached to the ninth-century Samanid dynasty as an antecedent; Kazakhstan made the new capital Astana the main symbol of the nation, and in Turkmenistan President Niyazov cast himself in that role in an elaborate personality cult.

Whatever the drafters of the Freedom Support Act thought they were doing, against this background of countries with insecure identities their actions were perceived as undermining the new governments rather than supporting them. In fairness, the Foreign Assistance Support Act did not preclude collaborations with the new governments—in fact, it explicitly allows support to official bodies—but the thrust of its provisions favor independent individuals and "civil society" groups as the most effective agents for advancing democracy. This set the U.S. at odds with the new governments from the outset.

Given the Freedom Support Act's stress on building electoral and parliamentary systems, one might have expected it also to have focused on the fair and effective administration of laws and public matters as a prerequisite of democracy. But in fact it makes no mention of governance as such. In the case of the post-Soviet states of Central Asia and the Caucasus, this neglect was especially regrettable. In addition to being a one-party system, the Soviet Union was a vast administrative state, involving millions of people who, to a greater or lesser degree, had accommodated themselves to the specific management culture of Communism. Thousands of offices, commissions, and agencies of every type regulated every aspect of citizens' lives. Meanwhile, the inherent contradictions and shortages produced by this model generated a profound corruption within all these institutions. Since scores of these Soviet-type agencies survived thanks to sheer momentum into the post-Soviet world, the new governments inherited countless and powerful administrative organs that were fundamentally incompatible with democracy. It was therefore inconceivable that democracy could advance without the transformation or abolition of such bodies. The framers of the Act ignored this, if they were conscious of it at all, and development assistance never made it a primary focus. They therefore saw little need to bring American expertise to bear on administrative reform, which was viewed as a lesser and inconsequential realm. One must assume they believed that the institution of something called democracy would ipso facto transform the inherited bureaucratic state, rather than the other way around. By this neglect, they passed up the chance to create an enabling environment for both democracy and economic development.

The Freedom Support Act was designed to advance market economies, security, and democracy equally across the entire former Soviet bloc. In practice, it distributed American largesse quite unequally. Favorites emerged from the outset and their privileged position was reflected in large differentials between USAID funding for projects by country. The first palpable difference is that the funds lavished on countries in the South Caucasus were considerable larger than what was disbursed in Central Asia. These differentials emerged early and persist to the present. Thus, Georgia received $1.38 billion in USAID assistance between 2001 and 2013, not counting several hundred million more from the Millennium Challenge Corporation. Armenia followed with $671 million, with Azerbaijan receiving considerably less, at $269 million. In Central Asia, by far the largest recipient of USAID project support was Kyrgyzstan, which received a total of ca. $460 million in the fifteen years beginning in 2001. So favored was Kyrgyzstan in USAID's program that it alone has been designated a "stand-alone mission." By contrast, Turkmenistan, which has a population roughly the same size as Kyrgyzstan's (5.8 million vs. 5.3 million), received only $83 million, barely a fifth as much.

The reason for this dramatic gap is that Kyrgyzstan was perceived as being democratic – "the Switzerland of Central Asia," in the words of its publicity-savvy first president, Askar Akayev – while Turkmenistan, where one-man authoritarianism prevailed, was not. This bias persisted in spite of the short-lived thuggish regime in Kyrgyzstan of Kurmanbek

Bakiyev in 2005-10, Kyrgyzstan's closing of the NATO base at Manas, its decision to join Vladimir Putin's Eurasian Union, and its mismanagement of the South of the country – where the relegation of ethnic Uzbeks to second-class citizens helped make it a notorious breeding ground for domestic and foreign Islamists.[9] Through all this runs the thread of corruption which, in the judgment of a Swedish expert on the subject, can no longer described as infecting the government but has, in functional terms, become the government: "In Kyrgyzstan, corruption is not a problem for the state, it *is* the state."[10] None of these concerns proved an impediment to the U.S. providing disproportionate support for Kyrgyzstan and for cutting back help to all its neighbors.

Turning to Kyrgyzstan's antipode, Turkmenistan, we find a country ruled by successive strong and idiosyncratic authoritarian leaders since 1992. Political and religious dissent are not tolerated and there is no functioning parliament. At the same time, this closed society has recently opened an international university where English is the language of instruction, and has allowed ten thousand students to go abroad, many on government-funded scholarships. It has worked stubbornly and effectively to advance the TAPI gas pipeline across Afghanistan to Pakistan and India, which will provide a crucial income stream to the government of Afghanistan, to whose maintenance America has sacrificed nearly three thousand of its young men and women and a trillion dollars of its wealth. Finally, Turkmenistan possesses what BP estimates to be 24.3 trillion cubic meters of gas reserves, equal to those of Qatar, and is bound to become a significant factor in European and world energy in the coming decades.[11] Notwithstanding these factors, the U.S. has been steady in its arms-length treatment of Turkmenistan; the EU has yet to ratify a Partnership and Cooperation Agreement with it, signed in 1998, which the European Parliament and certain member state resisted over human rights concerns.

A similar logic has been at work in the Caucasus, with added twists resulting from the work of domestic lobbies in the United States. Georgia has received by far the largest assistance of any country studied here, in fact more than double that of the runner-up, Armenia, and almost four times that of its neighbor, Azerbaijan, whose population is double that of Georgia. Again, the main criterion, especially before Azerbaijan acquired oil wealth, was the perceived divergence in democracy and human rights – with Georgia positioning itself as a "beacon of democracy." Yet Azerbaijan, while undoubtedly a more authoritarian state, is uniquely placed as a secular and pro-Western nation, with a majority population consisting of Shi'a Muslims—no trivial a matter in light of the anti-American theocracy that prevails across the border in Shi'a Iran. And while Armenia, a country of three million, occupies large areas of Azerbaijani territory, it has received double the amount of aid – almost six times more per capita – than Azerbaijan.

Let us pass over for now the question of what, in light of these realities, *should* be the policy of the U.S. towards Kyrgyzstan and Turk-menistan, or Georgia and Azerbaijan. Serious people can disagree on this complex issue. For now, let us simply note that U.S. policy towards these nations has been defined *not* by balancing the pros and cons in the areas of security, economics, and rights, but by basing the decision *solely* on one factor: their perceived stances on democracy and human rights.

Judgments regarding the worthiness or unworthiness of partic-ular countries were inevitably controversial. The Freedom Support Act empowers (but does not require) the President to withhold development assistance from countries where progress towards democracy is slow or nonexistent and where human rights violations are deemed common. Uz-bekistan, Turkmenistan and Azerbaijan have at different times been sin-gled out for their purported sins, and have seen U.S. support drastically curtailed. But in most cases decisions pro or con appear to have arisen from judgments that must be characterized as highly subjective.

Kazakhstan has received a total of $418.5 million over fifteen years, making it the second largest recipient of USAID funds in Central Asia, after tiny Kyrgyzstan. We would be the first to argue that Kazakh-stan has pursued many very enlightened policies, and has effectively es-tablished itself as an independent voice on the world scene, in spite of its membership in Putin's Eurasian Economic Union. But throughout the period in question, human rights NGOs criticized violations of personal and religious liberties purportedly committed by the government, while election monitoring teams sent by the Organization for Security and Co-operation in Europe (OSCE) raised questions about the process of elec-tions there. To be sure, other reviews made more positive evaluations of Kazakhstani elections. But political power there is rigorously centralized, with next to no local self-governance, and concentrated in the hands of the President for Life, Nursultan Nazarbayev. In short, Kazakhstan, like every other country in the region, presents a combination of pluses and minuses which defy the tidy conclusions of the State Department's Bureau of Democracy, Human Rights, and Labor.

Our purpose in citing these contradictory points is neither to crit-icize nor defend U.S. and European approaches to Kazakhstan. In fact, we consider them to have been positive. Rather, it is to question the rationality of the allocation process as a whole, which has resulted in striking anomalies that arise more from bureaucratic tugs-of war than from any rigorous process.

Even more striking than the unequal allocation of western support across Central Asia and the Caucasus are the broad variations in support *per capita* across the region. Georgia and Armenia have seen investments of $283 and $223 per capita, respectively, while Azerbaijan's figure is only $38. For Kyrgyzstan, the number is $79, while for Uzbekistan, the second most populous country in the region after Afghanistan, the corresponding figure is a mere $12. This figure can be explained in part - but only in part—by the U.S. government's acceptance of NGO reports, mainly from Human Rights Watch, that at Andijan in May 2005 Uzbek government troops fired on "unarmed civilians" and "especially pious Muslims," killing hundreds. Recent detailed research, backed by several films shot on the spot by the insurgents themselves, has confirmed that the "civilians" were in fact heavily armed, having overwhelmed a government arms depot and stolen its contents, and that the "especially pious Muslims" were in fact Islamist militants who planned the event as a show of force against the government.[12] The same findings confirm the government's tally of those killed at about 187-211, of which scores were shot by the insurgents and others died because the insurgents used them as human shields. In this case, the State department and USAID appear to have rushed to judgment, without rigorously testing the evidence upon which that judgment was based.

Thus, a confusion built into the Freedom Support Act was over whether U.S. support should be handed out on the basis of need or as a reward for progress achieved by the new governments. Their non-solution was to opt for both, focusing security assistance on countries that had a demonstrated need for it and handing out economic and democracy-building funds on countries that seemed, in Washington's judgment, to be making progress in those areas. This bifurcation was clearly built into the Act's mandate, when it instructs the President to take into account "the extent to which the independent state is taking action to make significant progress towards, and is committed to, the comprehensive implementation of a democratic system based on principles of the rule of law, individual freedoms, and representative government determined by free and fair election."

Viewing the wide differentials of U.S. support for new countries in the Caucasus and Central Asia, four conclusions are warranted: first, that the differences are the result of many individually small decisions that have been compounded over time; second, that the State Department and USAID have viewed disbursements under the Freedom Support Act mainly as bonuses for what they perceive as good behavior rather than as investments in a secure, economically open, and democratic future; third, that population sizes and the geopolitical importance of countries have played at best a secondary role in allocation decisions, leading to great largesse lavished on a few countries and the virtual neglect of others; and fourth, that overall balances have never been subject to rigorous review and evaluation by the bureaucracies in Washington, Brussels and other European capitals.

Indeed, this problem was not limited to the United States: the EU and European states over time became even more explicit in their bifurcation of countries into those it considered to be good or bad students. Individual countries chose to focus almost exclusively on one or another country: thus, for example, Sweden became a major donor to Georgia on account of its undeniable progress from 2003 onward, while closing down its activities in Central Asia, and maintaining some programs in Armenia while shunning Azerbaijan. Again, the sole criterion was the perception of democratic progress. The same logic led Sweden to become the largest bilateral donor to Moldova for several years in the 2000s; but this enthusiasm turned into deep frustration when it emerged that Moldova's pro-European coalition was no less corrupt than its pro-Russian counterparts, and avidly mismanaged the country and the considerable European assistance offered it.[13]

A 2013 EU document explicitly explains the "more for more" principle, in which the EU "offers our neighbours a privileged relationship, building upon a mutual commitment to common values" and "will develop stronger partnerships with those neighbours that make more progress towards democratic reform."[14] The EU often used directly divisive language: in December 2013, EU Commissioner Stefan Füle announced additional aid to Armenia, Moldova and Georgia by noting that "three Eastern partners were rewarded for their efforts in democratic transition and their commitment to fundamental values."[15] Thus, the EU explicitly divides its neighbors into better and worse categories. While this may have been intended as a form of carrot-and stick approach that would lead other countries to follow suit, there is no evidence this has been the consequences of the practice. Quite to the contrary, one suspects that its main effect was to alienate those countries not found worthy of "rewards". Inadvertently, the American and European approach has contributed to exacerbating differences and deepening the gulf between these states.

While the selective treatment of countries *within* the region is an important matter, an even more fundamental issue arises when comparing Western policy toward these countries with American and European approaches to the rest of the world. The fact that American and European policies post-1991 were rooted in the Helsinki accords means that standards were applied to these countries that have not been applied elsewhere. This goes back to the assumptions of the "Transition Paradigm", discussed in chapter 3: because Western states assumed that all states in transition from communism were in transition toward liberal democracy, their performance since then has been held to that higher standard. The Helsinki-era CSCE was turned into the OSCE, which among other made it a practice to send observation teams to elections in all former Communist countries to monitor their compliance with "OSCE standards," shorthand for the standards of the most advanced Western states. As discussed below, this ensured most post-Soviet states, dealing with a Soviet institutional legacy, were always found wanting.

This may have made sense for the countries that sought rapid integration into the European and Euro-Atlantic institutions like the EU and NATO, which require certain conditions are met regarding governance. But twenty-five years later, it has long since become clear that the EU and NATO are not about to open their doors to the countries of Central Asia and the Caucasus; neither are those states, with the sole exception of Georgia, overtly campaigning for full integration into those bodies. This raises the question why the U.S. and European states should continue to see the entirety of their relations with Central Asian and South Caucasian countries primarily through the prism of their performance in the field of democratic development and human rights. Certainly, this is not the case for countries like Vietnam and Saudi Arabia, close partners of the U.S. that have considerably more problematic records than the states covered in this book. Neither is it the case for Turkey – a member of NATO and a country that is technically in negotiations for EU membership. Following the massive crackdown on dissent in Turkey after the failed July 2016 coup against President Erdoğan, this application of different yardsticks has become glaring. America has long followed a policy of avoiding involvement in domestic Turkish matters; and in Europe, policy-makers overtly state that the importance of Turkey for the fight against ISIS or the migration crisis is such that it limits European ability to criticize Turkey for its rapid descent into authoritarian one-man rule. We do not dispute the validity of these concerns, or the policy choices of Western leaders. Serious people can disagree on these issues. But when the U.S. simultaneously makes human rights a key focus in its relations with states like Azerbaijan or Uzbekistan, its credibility seriously suffers, and that inevitably invites allegations of the application of double standards. It is increasingly common in the region for Western rhetoric on human rights not to be taken seriously. Regional leaders increasingly view such rhetoric as attempts by Western leaders to exert pressure for ulterior reasons, or simply as going after smaller countries to score a point with domestic constituencies while holding their tongue on the similar or worse abuses by larger powers like Russia or Turkey, which the West does not want to anger.

THE INFORMATION SPHERE

The drafters of the Freedom Support Act carried out their work in a fog of generalizations, some of them warranted and others quite without basis. Most striking was their near-total ignorance of the specifics of Soviet life and political culture. Curiously, the Act authorized the expenditure of billions of dollars to bring about change in the new states, but without providing any feedback channels for authoritative information on how the locals responded to Washington's ministrations. Nor were there any such provisions in EU programs. Maybe they assumed that officers in the newly opened Western embassies would provide such feedback, or that the State Department's research office – or analogous bodies in Europe – would do so. But the former lacked the staff to evaluate and verify evidence brought to them by the human rights lobby and the latter were busy with other matters. In short, the framers of the Act built into it no mechanism for mid-course corrections.

Arguably the most fundamental and devastating lacuna in the Freedom Support Act was its utter neglect of the sphere of information. Both regions, and indeed all former parts of the USSR, urgently needed to effect a transition from a limited and tightly controlled access to global sources of news and information to an open system in which western or American perspectives and values would be adequately represented. The framers surely knew that the Soviet system had struggled to squelch all independent sources of information, including those from the West, and that neither democratic politics nor an open economy would be possible without pluralism in the media. But they showed absolutely no awareness of this. Nor did they do anything to address this urgent need for access to global news and information. Instead they left the entire matter to the two radio stations operated by the United States Information Agency and a handful of underfunded cultural attaches in America's embassies. As a result, down to the present the main alternative to television controlled directly or indirectly by the new regional governments is Russian radio and TV. Indeed, Russian media continue to this day to dominate the airwaves. With the rise of Putin, these media became more than ever an arm of Moscow's policies in the region. That they often work hand in hand with local governments or investors makes matters worse. Print media is not similarly controlled everywhere, but newspapers, too, are dominated by stories fed them by Russian sources. Even where there is greater pluralism of information, as in Georgia or Kyrgyzstan, Russian sources still dominate the scene. And even the new and more independent print and electronic outlets suffer from the poor quality of their journalism – an issue largely neglected by western assistance programs.

A further impediment to a USAID role in information is that its leaders, and those of Radio Liberty and Voice of America, failed to grasp the urgency of the world media revolution taking place concurrently with the collapse of the USSR. In fact, no agency of the U.S. government was addressing this crucial issue. At a time when international news media were developing programming in heretofore neglected languages, and when communications satellites were being raised everywhere, this oversight was all the more serious. The closest the West came to this issue were a Eumetsat (European Organization for the Exploitation of Meteorological Satellites) for meteorological data and a regional satellite system proposed by the American (formerly Soviet) physicist Roald Sagdeev.

It was not the task of the drafters of the Freedom Support Act to anticipate every challenge that might arise as programs were implemented, but one problem should not have escaped their attention: corruption. By 1991, few topics concerning Russia and the USSR were more widely known and discussed in Washington than the rampant corruption there. The 1982 book *U.S.S.R., The Corrupt Society: The Secret World of Soviet Capitalism* by ex-Soviet lawyer Konstantin M. Simis opened the floodgate to a torrent of articles and studies on the subject. The CIA's National Intelligence Daily had long-since pelted its readers with titillating news on corruption across the USSR, and TV newscasters turned to it whenever other stories were lacking. Yet the drafters of the Freedom Support Act were either naïve or ignorant about this, or they assumed that corruption would magically vanish with the collapse of Soviet rule. They were wrong, as were their counterparts in Georgia and their oversight left the U.S. government helpless before an army of grant recipients, more than a few of whom mastered the art of gaming Western Capitals.

THE CULTURAL FACTOR

In terms of cultural geography, both the Freedom Support Act, USAID and European governments took the position that for all their cultural differences, the new post-Communist governments in the Baltic, Eastern Europe, the Caucasus and Central Asia all faced pretty much the same problems as they entered the post-Soviet era, and should therefore be lumped together organizationally. The goal, in the words of the Act, was "to unlock Cold War restrictions, which applied everywhere." While this is quite logical, it grossly underestimated the profoundly different experience of the Baltic and Central European countries, which had been independent between the wars and had always viewed themselves as part of Europe, and the Caucasus and Central Asia, which had radically different cultures and had endured seven decades of Soviet rule. All regions had experienced communist rule, but the differences between them demanded a difference in the application of American assistance that the Act did not provide for. Moreover, it applied the same "one size fits all" approach equally to the Caucasus, which include two Christian peoples and a Shiite nation, and to Sunni Central Asia. Only gradually did the governments of the U.S. and Europe come to acknowledge this and begin to adjust their structures accordingly.

As has been noted, the Act did not provide funds for the research necessary to the development of sound policies, especially in the area of democratization and human rights. As a result, inadequate research on the part of the State Department has been responsible for painting some regional countries in brighter colors than is warranted, and other countries in darkly sinister hues. An example of this is the West's differential treatment of those societies that had inherited recent traditions of nomadism and those that had been formed over the centuries by the demands of irrigated oasis agriculture. The former, notably Kazakhstan and Kyrgyzstan, had long been organized mainly along horizontal lines, with small units functioning quite independently and interacting only occasionally with national tribal leaders and authorities. The latter, notably Uzbekistan and Tajikistan, had lived for centuries under the stark need to maintain complex irrigation systems, which in turn demanded for their strong, centralized, and vertical systems of command and control. Ignorant of these realities or choosing to ignore them, western donor countries and foundations systematically favored the former over the latter. Worse, they assumed that the "hydraulic" societies labored under some undefined pathology that had to be removed before real progress would be possible.

USAID and analogous bodies in Europe then proceeded to use these judgments – exaggerated, imperfect, and in some cases simply wrong – to justify the extension or withholding of western largesse. No wonder that many in the region see America and Europe, in their distribution of development assistance funds, like capricious young girls, handing out posies or withholding them from beaux as they pass through the crowd. Particularly conspicuous in USAID's decisions on who should, or should not, receive assistance money, was the absolute primacy of "progress towards democracy and the protection of human rights" as the overriding factor for its calculus, without any adjustment for social and cultural realities on the ground. Let it be noted here that America, Great Britain and France present contrasts in the area of decentralization, governmentalization, and self- government that are no less fundamental or dramatic than those between, say, Kazakhstan/Kyrgyzstan and Uzbekistan/Tajikistan. Yet all of these certifiably "Western" states, in spite of their differences, are considered today to be true democracies.

THE PROBLEM OF COORDINATION

This, then, brings us to the most important, and at the same time, the most vexing issue, namely, how do the three priorities—security, economic development, and democracy/human rights—relate to each other on the ground in each country and in the region? Let us admit at the outset that this is no simple challenge. It is similar to that posed by chess for a person who has heretofore played only checkers. It is like a three-part fugue for a musician who is accustomed to playing simple melodies. Yet it cannot be avoided. Actually, one *can* sidestep it, but at the price of the kind of confusion in U.S. and European policy that actually exists today. Indeed, far the most significant shortcoming of the Freedom Support Act was its failure to provide for adequate coordination between the three "baskets" from which the U.S. dispensed assistance to the region.

To be sure, the Act provided for a "coordinator" from the Department of State, whose job is not only to "design overall assistance" to the states of the former Soviet Union but also "to assure coordination among all agencies [of the U.S. Government] that are involved," "resolve policy and program disputes among U.S. Government agencies with respect to U.S. assistance for the independent states," and even to "ensure the proper management, implementation, and oversight by the agencies."[16] But the Act failed to assign a sufficiently lofty rank to this official, and created no regular and high-level inter-agency body to effect the required coordination. There was no explicit provision or support for the interagency process that is essential for any of the many areas where coordination is called for.

As a result, this vital task was consigned to a subordinate officer within the Department of State, who is three levels down from the Secretary of State, and who coordinates with other agencies on an infrequent and *ad hoc* basis and with no power to harmonize the various programs. Even within the Department of State itself coordination is weak. Note that the office of Coordinator is housed in the Bureau of European and Eurasian Affairs, but from February 2006, the five Central Asian countries were shifted to the Bureau of South and Central Asian Affairs. Moreover, the Bureau of Democracy, Human Rights and Labor has taken strong and unilateral initiatives in the region in its area of responsibility; and in 2011, a new Bureau of Energy Resources was created. It is no secret that the different Bureaus often have fundamentally different perspectives on the countries in the region.

The inevitable consequence of this confusion was a tidal wave of criticism of security projects in countries deemed not to be making progress towards democracy and less public but nonetheless constant criticism of the near-total ban on support for countries deemed of central importance to regional security and the U.S.' security interests. Suffice it to say that in the period 2010-2014 Kyrgyzstan received two dollars per capita for democracy building and Uzbekistan nine cents.[17] This, in spite of the fact that Kyrgyzstan was being generously paid for the use of its Manas base while Uzbekistan, whose central location inevitably made it the keystone to regional security and American interests, received nothing for the use of its Kharshi-Khanabad base, as is the U.S. "usual" practice. Given this, it was scarcely surprising that the Uzbek government closed the U.S./NATO base at Khanabad while Kyrgyzstan, as noted above, experienced a second bloody revolution in 2010, closed the U.S./NATO base at Manas, and allowed its southern provinces to become an important base for Jihadists.

The lack of coordination between security and other concerns is particularly evident in the Freedom Support Act's treatment of religiously-inspired terrorism. The U.S. Government was acutely conscious of this issue by time the Act was drafted, thanks to the Beirut barracks attack of 1983, actions by the Islamic mujahidin in Afghanistan, and deeds of the Ayatollah Khomeini's security service during the Iran-Iraq war from 1980 to 1988. Indeed, fear of Iran-style Islamic extremism was one of the U.S.'s principal security concerns in Central Asia and the Caucasus at the time the Freedom Support Act was being drafted. Yet the Act is silent on the U.S.'s support for secular governments based on secular systems of law, and for secular education. These important affirmations and concerns found no place in either the democracy or human rights basket, for the purviews of both had been specified in such a way as to exclude such security concerns as religious extremism or terrorism.

MANDATES RATHER THAN AGREEMENTS

One final aspect of the Freedom Support Act that warrants our attention here is important because it conditioned everything that followed: the law was a one-sided action by Congress and signed by the President, and was not supplemented by comprehensive intergovernmental agreements. Such comprehensive intergovernmental agreements could clearly spell out the reciprocal obligations that any recipient of U.S. largesse would assume as a condition of the aid. Indeed, this is exactly what the European Union has aspired to do in its Rule of Law programs in Central Asia, and to an even higher degree in the framework of the Eastern Partnership.

Even as a normal law, the Freedom Support Act could have specified the positive steps that recipient governments should take in order to receive support under any of the three baskets. Lacking this, the only provision in the text is a section empowering the President to withhold money or cut off aid entirely to any country "whom [he] deems is engaged in a consistent pattern of gross violations of internationally recognized human rights or of international law."[18] This "all or nothing" approach was to have predictable consequences.

Implementation of the Freedom Support Act began as soon President Bush signed it into law on October 24, 1992. The Department of State turned at once to the United States Agency for International Development (USAID) to implement certain of the programs mandated by the Freedom Support Act. Formed to implement the Foreign Assistance Act of 1961, USAID immediately opened offices in all countries of the Caucasus and Central Asia, including Azerbaijan, which was banned by Section 907 from receiving direct government-to-government support under the Freedom Support Act.

USAID is a capacious agency, spending its $35 billion budget for 2015 in more than hundred countries.[19] And while it fully embraced Freedom Support Act goals in the area of economic development and human rights, it had its own agenda as well. These further commitments included support for health systems, hunger and disaster relief, and access to education. Over the years USAID's worldwide agenda was further broadened to include mitigating the impact of climate change and fostering gender equality, all of which it advanced in Central Asia and the Caucasus. Although its senior staff includes a large number of Foreign Service Officers, and although USAID maintains a close working relationship with the State Department, it is an independent agency, whose Administrator is confirmed by Congress and reports directly to Congress.

USAID participates in the definition of the U.S.'s foreign assistance policies and budgets. But the Secretary of State, National Security Council, or President can quickly reorient long-standing priorities, as occurred when President Obama designated the eradication of extreme poverty globally as a prime development goal. Such changes inevitably affect all other budgets. Moreover, because USAID carries out programs for many departments besides State, and because USAID itself has developed programs that require years, or even decades, to complete, the focus on any single piece of legislation like the Freedom Support Act is likely to be diluted by other priorities and not to endure for long. The existence of *both* geographical and functional bureaus, while typical of major international aid and financial organizations, creates further inevitable challenges, this time of coordination.

The involvement of multiple agencies of the U.S. government in closely related issues and countries brings advantages in terms of flexibility and adaptability, but it greatly complicates the work of coordinating among them. Even the most diligent Coordinator of Assistance to Europe and Eurasia could not keep abreast of the multitude of overlapping projects in Central Asia and the Caucasus, let alone provide the strategic planning called for in the Act. As we will see in Chapter 6, the broad definition of their missions adopted by USAID and OPIC enabled them to support Freedom Support Act goals but at the same time to extend the U.S. government's overall commitments in Central Asia and the Caucasus far beyond what was foreseen by that legislation. This is notably the case with the principle of "good governance," which a number of USAID initiatives have advanced, notwithstanding the Freedom Support Act's silence on the subject. Unfortunately, amidst the prevailing lack of clarity and coordination, what might be considered a positive move has only added to the prevailing confusion over ends and means.

SECURITY ASSISTANCE WITHOUT SECURITY

The same can be said of the Act's third basket, security. The Pentagon set about implementing the provisions of the Act in that sphere, working alone and in consort with the North Atlantic Treaty Organization (NATO). In 1993 the U.S. Secretary of Defense proposed to fellow NATO members to establish a "Partnership for Peace" with the new states formed from the collapsed Soviet Union, for the purpose of professionalizing their military, modernizing their policy planning, training, and governmental relations and coordinating them with NATO, and advancing environmental projects and disaster planning. A region-wide NATO Liaison Officer with offices first in Kazakhstan and then in Uzbekistan was set up to engage regional countries in cooperative programs with NATO. At NATO's Istanbul Summit in 2004 Allied leaders decided to make partnership with Central Asia and the Caucasus a priority for the Alliance. Tellingly, it stated that 'NATO sees no contradiction between [the cooperation of regional countries] with the Alliance and their desire to build strong relations with other organizations."[20] Parallel with this, with defense attaches at all its embassies in the Caucasus and Central Asia, the Pentagon proved effective in its ability to advance the "security basket" of the Freedom Support Act.

This was achieved through training programs for senior officers and the provision of modern skills and equipment to the regional armed forces. All countries in the region participated with the exception of Turkmenistan, which cited its permanently neutral status as a reason. In a few short years military cultures that had been saturated with the primitive values of the Red Army's began to change and evolve. Uzbekistan appointed Kadyr Gulyamov Minister of Defense, the first civilian to hold that position in the former Soviet Union. A scientist by training, Gulyamov promptly launched massive retraining programs at bases throughout the country. In Georgia, the Pentagon from 2001 onward launched a Train-and-Equip Program that turned the Georgian armed forces, previously in a dilapidated condition, into a professional and competent military force.

However, NATO everywhere refused to provide training or other services to forces under Ministries of Internal Affairs on the grounds that they were really police and should not be treated as military. It is worth noting that the Uzbek "military" forces that were on the ground during the bloody events at Andijan in May 2005 were old Red Army-type units from the Ministry of Internal Affairs that had not been subjected to NATO reform initiatives, unlike units of the regular Army that had undergone NATO retraining.

The launch of NATO's military campaign in Afghanistan in 2001 sharply realigned NATO's interests in Central Asia, viewing them thereafter mainly, in its own words, "through an Afghan lens."[21] This meant using the region as a transport corridor and supply depot for the support of ISAF forces in Afghanistan, a mission that was achieved through bases which NATO leased at Manas, Kyrgyzstan, Khanabad, Uzbekistan, and through the Northern Distribution Network (NDN) extending from the

Baltic through Latvia and Russia and then through Kazakhstan and Uzbekistan to Afghanistan. The Caucasus provided a second corridor for supplies, thanks to overflight rights granted by Azerbaijan and Georgia. While there was endless talk of procuring needed goods in Central Asia rather than bringing them from America or Europe, restrictive rules on procurement prevented this from happening. What could have been a boon to the economies of Central Asia became instead a colossal and wasteful drain on western economies.

For a half decade after 2002 Afghanistan claimed most of NATO's and the U.S.'s energies in Central Asia and the Caucasus. However, Russia's invasion of Georgia in August, 2008, reminded everyone that the regional states had security concerns that were quite independent of Afghanistan. What could states in the Caucasus and Central Asia expect from NATO in the event of a threat to their borders? The best NATO could come up with was the Partnership for Peace's Framework Document, which enshrines the Allies' commitment "to consult with any partner country that perceives a threat to its territorial integrity."[22] When Russian meddling in Georgia's unresolved conflicts grew worse from 2002 onward, the Government of Georgia launched a campaign to gain full membership in NATO. Other regional states saw this move as risky or quixotic and began carefully calibrating their security arrangements in terms not of *alignment* but of *balance* among external powers. Similarly, the PfP Partnership Agreement had obliged signatories to respect existing borders and refrain from force or the threat of force. Would NATO apply this in the case of Armenia's occupation of a sixth of the territory of Azerbaijan? It chose not to do so.

OUTSOURCING

It was clear from the outset that existing agencies of the State Department, Pentagon and other U.S. government agencies had neither the expertise nor the time to handle the many separate programs that comprised the three "baskets." And so began a process of what later became known as "outsourcing," i.e., farming out the implementation to a series of quasi-independent and even private agencies.

In this spirit, Congress created and endowed the independent Eurasia Foundation to promote democratic reform, civil society, and entrepreneurship across the region. Its first director had headed the staff of the Senate Foreign relations Committee. It also set up a Central Asia Investment Fund to invest in start-up firms, and a parallel fund for the Caucasus. In implementing the Act, Congress in some cases modified the original legislation. For example, the Act had specified the creation of a "Democracy

Corps" to fund, organize, fund, and monitor "Democracy Houses" across the region. In recognition that Republicans and Democrats may see the promotion of democracy differently, Congress instead supported the National Democratic Institute and International Republican Institute, and the Democracy Houses were quietly abandoned. This arrangement led inevitably to overlapping projects and sometimes costly inefficiencies, as well as to confusion in recipient countries.

The role of outsourcing was particularly notable in the case of the democratization and human rights baskets. One of the tasks foreseen by the drafters was the monitoring of national elections throughout Central Asia and the Caucasus. Not only did the State Department lack staff to do this but it prudently understood that its judgments might be subject to challenges from unfriendly quarters. In practice, it therefore outsourced the monitoring of elections – primarily to the Organization for Security and Cooperation in Europe, but the National Democratic Institute and International Republican Institute have also fielded their own, parallel election observation missions. The OSCE, a multi-national structure of initially thirty-five countries, had been formed as the Conference on Security and Cooperation in Europe in 1973 as part of the East-West negotiating process that led to the Helsinki agreement. Turned into an Organization in 1994, the OSCE's mission anticipated many aspects of the Freedom Support Act, and by the early 1990s it had begun monitoring elections in the new countries of the post-Soviet world.

In both the economic and security baskets much of the outsourcing was carried out not by not-for-profit NGOs but by private for-profit firms, mainly based in the Washington area and for the most part led, if not staffed, by former employees of the Pentagon or Commerce Department. Typical of these entities was Macfadden, a Silver Spring, Maryland firm founded in 1986 "for mission critical support in the areas of international disaster response, development and humanitarian assistance, information technology solutions, financial management systems support and knowledge management and communications." In spite of this broad mission, Macfadden was considered a small business at the time it applied for its first contract in 2006, which greatly enhanced its attractiveness to the State Department's Coordinator of Assistance to Europe and Eurasia. By 2009, however, its contract was threatened by its loss of its classification as a small business. Macfadden therefore partnered with another Beltway firm, Blue-Force, and was able to continue its work in behalf of the Freedom Support Act.

The range of tasks outsourced to just this one firm is impressive, to say the least. As stated in its own literature, the company was contracted, "to provide program, budget, and foreign affairs professional experts to assist in the interagency coordinator of U.S. economic, democracy, security, and law enforcement, and other U.S. government assistance. In addition, the team will provide information technology support, program planning and performance measurement, and logistics planning and facilitation support for the operation of the evaluation teams."[23]

With due respect for the talents of Macfadden's and BlueForce's personnel, one wonders how any small firm could so quickly assemble the necessary skill to carry out these diverse tasks, let alone with even a modicum of awareness of, and sensitivity to, the complex political and social environment of the Caucasus and Central Asia. Maybe this is irrelevant, as the same firm boasts of similar contracts with the U.S. Coast Guard, Department of the Interior, and Department of the Treasury, among others.

Leaving this quibble aside, the practice of outsourcing all but guarantees the mutual isolation of such contracting firms from one another and from the other private, governmental, and not-for-profit agencies charged with implementing the Freedom Support Act. Indeed, given the competitive nature of bids, it directly encourages efforts by different grantees to undercut or undermine each other, as countless stories by expats in the region confirm. Under such conditions, is it realistic even to speak of coordinating the effort as a whole? Finally, it should be noted that the cost of such outsourcing is very high, involving overhead fees in some cases up to seventy percent of the base cost.

Outsourcing in this and several other cases brought unanticipated problems. OSCE teams did highly professional jobs of studying and reporting the course of elections across the Caucasus and Central Asia. But its guidelines required that all reports begin with a direct statement that the election in question either did, or did not, meet the standards of the OSCE. Since OSCE was comprised mainly of European countries, many with long-established traditions of national elections, it was a foregone conclusion in most, if not all, cases that the election in question would fail to meet OSCE standards. It would have been an easy matter to change this requirement to state simply if the given election was an improvement or step backwards from the previous election. But neither the U.S. nor any other OSCE member thought of this. As a result, the OSCE gained a negative reputation for wagging its finger in judgment like an old-fashioned school master; the United States, as the OSCE's biggest and richest member, was assumed to be behind these public and very humiliating dressing downs.

A further and especially important instance of outsourcing concerned the democratization and human rights basket. No other area of U.S. involvement in Central Asia and the Caucasus was, and is, more sensitive than this, and more politically volatile both in the region and in the U.S. itself. Under the circumstances, it would be particularly important to make sure that the U.S. government was always acting on the basis of authoritative and unbiased information, the veracity of which it had tested and verified. Yet from the outset, funding for the Freedom Support Act was starkly inadequate to this task. As a result, the Department of State effectively outsourced these areas to non-governmental organizations such as Freedom House and Human Rights Watch. While generally conscientious in their work, such groups can easily become agents of special interest political lobbies, and indeed they are labeled as such by such respected publications as *The Economist.*

The implementation of the Freedom Support Act has been rich with anomalies. Among these, none is more striking than U.S. support for democracy. Among the most commonly-heard criticisms is that the U.S. and, to a lesser but still significant extent, European states, have focused a disproportionate amount of their resources and energies on "democracy promotion." Yet neither the Caucasus nor Central Asia, with the partial exception of Georgia and Kyrgyzstan, can claim any marked gains in this area since independence. Authoritarianism, not democracy, remains the region-wide norm. Nor is this surprising, for the hopes of the initial post-Soviet era have given way to a worldwide erosion and decline of democratic institutions.[24] And for all the talk of democracy and human rights in the Helsinki Final Act and in the Freedom Support Act, neither the U.S. nor EU has spent much money on it. Between the years 2009-2016 funding on both sides of the Atlantic was flat.[25] To be sure, the fact that Congress increased the budget for National Endowment for Democracy budget from $115 million to $170 million between 2009 and 2016 partially qualifies this statistic. And Thomas Carothers makes a valid point when he argues that in the same years, U.S. programs have improved by redirecting their efforts from top leaders in the capitals to other relevant actors country-wide.[26] Nonetheless, it is clear that the promotion of democracy, effective or not, has been, and remains a relatively minor element of the overall aid budget. As Larry Diamond puts it, "One of the biggest challenges facing democracy today is that its biggest champion – the United States – has lost interest in promoting it."[27]

The same charge is even more valid for the promotion of effective governance, i.e., the development of responsive and effective governmental institutions and the preparation of qualified people to staff them. This has been the implied purpose of countless programs mounted by the U.S. and EU in both the Caucasus and Central Asia, but it remains quite marginal in the awareness of elites on either side of the Atlantic and in the budgets they approve. In a later chapter we will argue that progress in the area of "good governance" is an absolute prerequisite for democracy and also for respect for human rights, and that programs in this area should be significantly expanded in the years to come.

The problem of replication of programs and of coordination among them is multiplied when the activities of the European Union and its member states are taken into account. Beginning shortly after the passage of the Freedom Support Act in the U.S., European assistance quickly mushroomed to involve nearly as large a number of institutions and organizations as their counterparts in America. Great Britain, Germany, Sweden, Finland, Switzerland and the Netherlands were particularly active, each of them mounting programs of their own; the EU, as mentioned, subsequently became a key donor in its own right. Added to this are the innumerable projects of the World Bank and EBRD, all discussed at length in the previous chapter. Thanks to this, it is not unusual to have the U.S., EU, separate countries, and both the World Bank and EBRD all mounting projects in the same general area. This exists, for example, in water management. In this and other areas where duplication and overlap exists, it is the local partners who suffer, for they sometimes find themselves the sole linkage among the various funders.

Beyond the lack of coordination is the problem of monitoring the proliferating assistance projects. Whether public, private, or for-profit, each American and European initiative formed local partnerships in each country in the region. The result is an extremely complex and utterly confusing skein of relationships. Suffice it to say that Switzerland alone entered into formal partnerships with some forty-five separate governmental entities in the Caucasus alone. It goes without saying that it is beyond the capacities of the sponsors to stay abreast of these links, let alone monitor their effectiveness. As we have seen, nearly all Western programs opened themselves wide to corruption on the part of local partners. Indeed, in practically every country, but more blatantly so in favored countries like Georgia and Kyrgyzstan, a whole class of "aid grantsmen" emerged, moving deftly from one contract to the next, updating their resumes to indicate their absolute mastery of each newly funded field.

IGNORING SECULARISM
In 1998 Congress established the US International Commission on Reli-

gious Freedom (USCIRF). In recent reports, the Commission appears to focus its activities in Central Asia and the Caucasus on protecting the rights of Islamic extremists. Among the issues that it has chosen to advocate are the right of mullahs from the Gulf states and Iran to work in moderate Muslim countries and, not least, to castigate countries that ban head covering of girls in public schools. The accuracy of the USCIRF reports is also suspect. As noted above, USCIRF does not pretend to conduct original research, relying instead on reports of international and local NGOs. Thus, USCIRF recycles the reports of other organizations and puts the stamp of the U.S. Government on them, without independently verifying their accuracy. Furthermore, USCIRF reports provide no references to the sources of their data. No credible scientific publication would ever reach publication without verifiable data. With only a dozen regular staff members, it is clear that the USCIRF does not possess the language capacity or expertise to truly understand the intricacies of church-state relations around the globe.

The USCIRF is particularly harsh in its condemnation of the Muslim-majority states in Central Asia and Azerbaijan. Adhering to the French secularist model of *laïcité*, these countries base their laws on constitutional principles and not on the *sharia* or Islamic principles. In bright contrast to the Middle East, non-Muslims there can live as equal citizens and with freedom of religion. Equally important, these states protect secular citizens, including women, from religious coercion. Yet, the Commission regularly declares these states in violation of religious freedom, largely because Islamic extremists who would like to overturn this order and enforce a religious state are not given the space to operate freely.

The USCIRF has condemned Tajikistan for legislation that requires the registration of religious institutions and studies. Sharing a long and porous border with Afghanistan, Tajikistan is concerned that terrorists from Afghanistan do not operate under the guise of religious activity. The USCIRF also condemned Tajikistan for a law that prohibits minors from engaging in religious activity without their parents' presence – a law intended to protect vulnerable young people from falling under the sway of extremists. Similarly, Uzbekistan has been censored for reviewing religious literature from abroad before approving it for distribution. Tashkent indeed filters out literature that violates the moderate community norms of this overwhelmingly Muslim society, and seeks to prevent the recurrence of the kind of extremist events that led to the deaths of hundreds. Should it not do so?

The USCIRF also complains that the school uniforms used in public schools in Azerbaijan do not allow hijab head covering of girls. France and Turkey have similar legislation (Turkey's was changed in 2014, however) yet the U.S. government has showed respect for their laws and customs. Moreover, the European Court of Human Rights has upheld countries' right to prohibit head scarves in schools, up to and including at the university level in Turkey. One cannot help wonder why a U.S. Government body criticizes Azerbaijan for policies sanctioned by the European Court of Human Rights and practiced by two of its closest allies. USCIRF has also condemned Azerbaijan's banning foreign citizens from serving as Muslim clerics there, a law enacted to prevent Iranian and other extremist clerics from breeding extremism.

The regional states are seeking to protect the right of believers and secularists and to advance inter-religious harmony against the onslaught of alien extremist ideologies. Our purpose is not to deny that they sometimes cast their nets too wide and too often err on the side of repression. This is well-documented. But USCIRF does not appear interested in the challenges these countries face, nor in working with them to strike the right balance. It ignores the fact that some of these states maintain very friendly relations with the U.S. and are amenable to U.S. concerns and advice on these issues, particularly if the U.S. would accept the premise of their policies while seeking to improve its implementation and reach. Such an approach would be much more effective than the USCIRF's finger-wagging report cards.

Concluding Notes

This, then, is a critique of American and European activities in Central Asia and the Caucasus. Over the succeeding decades, organizational changes have been introduced, as, for instance, when the EU instituted a Special Representative each for the Caucasus and Central Asia, and when the U.S. launched its C-5 + 1 annual regional convocation in Central Asia. Nonetheless, the general structure of U.S. and EU engagement with both Central Asia and the Caucasus remained largely intact throughout the first quarter century of their involvement there, and continues today.

This overview neglects scores of initiatives that have borne fruit. For example, a little-heralded program by USAID in Kazakhstan contributed significantly to the development of a real estate and housing market in that country, while others supported the formation of an independent Securities and Exchange Commission, assisted in opening the country's first private stock exchange, and promoted oversight of the nascent securities market. Yet another program in Kazakhstan and elsewhere addressed the costly and ineffective medical systems inherited from the Soviet Union. Far from being imposed from without, these programs were voluntary and elicited significant co-funding from regional governments. Similarly, in Uzbekistan USAID has worked with the government in Tashkent to set up credit unions, microfinance banks, women's health clinics, and tuberculosis monitoring programs, while it collaborated with Kyrgyzstan to introduce international accounting standards, a legal market for fertilizers and seed imports, and helped the National Bank to carry out its supervisory role of banks throughout the country. Tajikistan benefited from three score new drinking water systems, and an anti-polio program that vaccinated 95% of the population under five years of age, while in Turkmenistan USAID partnered with Chevron and other corporations to develop start-up companies for processing fruits and vegetables, and to modernize the energy and banking sectors.

What is the total value of assistance and development programs launched in Central Asia and the Caucasus by the U.S., EU, NATO, the World Bank, EBRD, and western philanthropies during that past quarter century, and of investments in the region made by American and European firms and individuals? Strange to say, no overall accounting of these expenditures yet exists. However, it is safe to say that the total is in the dozens of billions.

It goes without saying that virtually every program initiated by Americans or Europeans has its critics. Without pausing to evaluate them all, it must be noted that many of the sponsoring agencies and groups have been commendably self-critical and thorough in monitoring and evaluating their work. Dozens of detailed analyses exist, and in some cases formed the basis for changes and corrections that have been instituted.

While fully acknowledging the immensity of Western support and assistance to Central Asia and the Caucasus and the many concrete advances they achieved over a quarter century, let us reiterate some of the principal shortcomings identified above and some of their underlying assumptions.

These fall under nine headings:
- The West wrongly assumed that "civil society" is somehow autonomous and independent from government, whereas in normally functioning societies it depends on the existence of effective governance and enabling institutions.
- The transition paradigm assumed by both the U.S. and Europe severely underestimated the importance and complexity of building open, effective and uncorrupt state institutions. This failure has led to endless misunderstandings with local governments and numerous problems, especially in the area

of democratization, where mutual misunderstanding and mistrust have too often prevailed.

- The West has often held the new states of Central Asia and the Caucasus to a stiffer standard than it applies in other parts of the world, including Southeast Asia, the Middle East, and parts of Latin America.
- Ignorance or neglect of the cultural context and deep history of the peoples of Central Asia and the Caucasus has led the West into misunderstandings that could easily have been avoided. Thus, we noted how misunderstanding of the vertical political structure of traditionally oasis and settled agricultural societies (Azerbaijan, Uzbekistan, Tajikistan) as opposed to the more horizontal and open political structure of the former nomads (Kyrgyzstan and Kazakhstan) has led to policies and actions that have limited the West's effectiveness.
- The West has severely undervalued or ignored the importance of its own values, especially in the area of religion. By ignoring the importance of secular states and secular systems of law, the West has missed an important area of potential collaboration with regional countries and at times inadvertently become, an active opponents of secularism and enabler of Islamism. Recent events in Turkey, Egypt and elsewhere should long since have led to a rethinking of this issue. But this has not happened.
- The new countries of the Caucasus and Central Asia all being relatively small states, it has been a constant temptation for the West to deal with them more as objects to be manipulated on political or cultural chessboards than as sovereign subjects in their own right. As a result, both the EU and U.S. have too often negotiated "over the heads" of governments in Central Asia and the Caucasus, addressing what it considers the "big issues" with big powers.
- Down to the present, both Americans and Europeans have misread Russia's aims and actions with respect to both the Caucasus and Central Asia, and underestimate the existential threat to their sovereignty that Russian policies have posed.
- Because of this, they have also misunderstood—or completely ignored—the view of regional governments that the preservation of sovereignty and security is the sine qua non for the advancement of all other western goals. Acknowledging and

understanding the security concerns of the countries of Central Asia and the Caucasus is a precondition and the best lever for progress in the economies and democratization.

- Both the EU and U.S. have been slow to embrace a *regional* approach to both the Caucasus and Central Asia. Even though the EU and U.S. finally established regional consultations in both areas in recent years, they have yet to fill them with significant content. By contrast, both the Asia Development Bank and the World Bank have advanced much further towards regionalism, as has China's newly-formed Asian Infrastructure Investment Bank. Instead, both the U.S. and EU have unwittingly played regional states off against one another, picking winners and losers and failing to grasp the commonalities that should form the basis of sound policy.

- For all the positive steps they have taken with respect to these two important regions, the West has hobbled itself through impatience. It conveniently forgets the time that was necessary to rebuild Germany, Japan, South Korea and Taiwan and establish them as functioning democracies with open systems of law and government. Instead, they have conducted themselves like the impatient farmer who plants in May and then stalks the fields in June, pulling out seedlings to see how they are doing.

In the next chapter we shall seek to identity some of the structural issues that limit the effectiveness of western programs in the region, and then suggest steps by which they can be corrected, or at least their alleviated. The final chapter will identify strategic issues that require rethinking, suggest better alternatives, and present practical steps for implementing them.

ENDNOTES

1. Reminiscence of the author of an event held in November 1990.
2. Curt Tarnoff, "The Former Soviet Union and U.S. Foreign Assistance in 1992: The Role of Congress," Congressional Research Service, May 20, 2004, p. 3.
3. Tarnoff, p.9.
4. S.Frederick Starr, "Power Failure: American Policy in the Caspian', *The National Interest*, Spring 1997.
5. FREEDOM Support Act, "S.2532 — 102nd Congress (1992)." https://www.congress.gov/bill/102nd-congress/senate-bill/2532/text?q=%7B"-search"%3A%5B"Freedom+Support+Act+1992"%5D%7D&resultIndex=1
6. Thomas Carothers, "The End of the Transition Paradigm", *Journal of Democracy*, vol. 13 no. 1, 2002, pp. 5-21, at p. 8.
7. Seymour Martin Lipset, "Some Social Requisites of Democracy: Economic Development and Political Legitimacy." *American Political Science Review*, vol. 53 no. 1, 1959, pp. 69-105.
8. "Celebrating 10 Years of the Rule of Law Initiative", EU-Central Asia Rule of Law Platform, March 13, 2017. (http://ruleoflaw.eu/celebrating-10-years-of-rule-of-law-initiative/)
9. For a deeper study of Kyrgyzstan's predicament, see Shirin Akiner, *Kyrgyzstan 2010: Conflict and Context*, Silk Road Paper, Central Asia-Caucasus Institute, July 2016. (http://silkroadstudies.org/publications/silkroad-papers-and-monographs/item/13207)
10. Ferghana.Ru Information Agency, "In Kyrgyzstan, corruption is not a problem for the state, it IS the state," 30 December 2012. http://enews.fergananews.com/article.php?id=2735,.; also Johan Engvall, *The State as Investment Market: Kyrgyzstan in Comparative Perspective*, University of Pittsburgh Press, 2016.
11. Oilprice.com, "Turkmenistan's Proven Natural Gas Reserves Almost Doubled in New BP Review," July 20, 2012. Retrieved from: http://oilprice.com/Latest-Energy-News/World-News/Turkmenistans-Proven-Natural-Gas-Reserves-Almost-Doubled-in-New-BP-Review.html
12. Jeffry Hartman, *The May 2005 Andijan Uprising: What We Know* , Silk Road Paper, Central Asia-Caucasus Institute & Silk Road Studies Program, May 2016.
13. Theodor Tudoroiu, "Democracy and State Capture in Moldova", *Democratization*, vol. 22 no. 4, 2015.
14. European Neighborhood Policy Fact Sheet, Memo 236, 2013. (http://europa.eu/rapid/press-release_MEMO-13-236_en.htm)
15. 'More for more' principle in action – EU rewards Moldova, Georgia and Armenia with €87 million to boost reforms, 12 December 2013. (http://eap-csf.eu/en/news-events/news/more-for-more-principle-in-action-eu-rewards-moldova-georgia-and-armenia-with-%E2%82%AC87-million-to-boost-reforms/)
16. Freedom Support Act, sec. 102.
17. "U.S. Assistance to Europe and Eurasia: Fact Sheet and remarks by Alina L. Romanowski, Coordinator of U.S. Assistance to Europe and

Eurasia, Bureau of European and Eurasian Affairs, Statement before the House Foreign Affairs Committee, Sub-Committee on Europe, Eurasia, and Emerging Threats," June 16,2015. http://www.state.gov/p/eur/rls/rm/2015/jun/243914.htm and http://www.state.gov/p/eur/ace/c11609.htm

18. Freedom Support Act, sec. 104.
19. Tarnoff, "U.S. Agency for International Development (USAID): Background, Operations, and Issues," Congressional Research Service, July 21, 2015, p. 1
20. 'NATO-OTAN Backgrounder," NATO Public Diplomacy Division, Brussels, 2014, p.2.
21. "EU and Central Asia: The Two Elephants that Never Met," EUCAM Watch (EU-Central Asia Monitoring), 2012, No.11, p. 1.
22. *Ibid.*, p. 7.
23. Macfadden, Retrieved from: http://www.macf.com/contract-awards/macfadden-continues-to-support-the-us-department-of-states-office-of-the-coordinator-of-us-assistance-to-europe-and-eurasia-eur-ace-through-its-subcontract-with-blueforce.html
24. Larry Diamond, "Democracy in Decline," *Foreign Affairs*, July-August, 2016.
25. Ibid., p. 152.
26. Thomas Carothers has made this point in several major writings, including Funding Virtue: Civil Society Aid and Democracy Promotion (co-edited with Marina Ottaway), Carnegie Endowment for International Peace, 2000; and Democracy Policy Under Obama: Revitalization or Retreat?, Carnegie Report, January 2012.
27. Diamond, p. 152.

STRUCTURAL PROBLEMS AND THEIR SOLUTIONS

■

In considering the areas in which the West's approach to the Caucasus and Central Asia could have been more effective, it is useful to inquire into the nature and source of those shortcomings. The fact is that the inadequacies are the results of quite different causes, Because of this, their alleviation requires different kinds of action. While any simple taxonomy is bound to distort what is a complex reality, it is nonetheless possible to trace most of the various shortcomings to three quite different sources.

The first group include those that arose from features of formal legislation, in the case of the U.S., the Freedom Support Act of 1992. In such cases, the most direct means of correcting the problem is either to amend or replace the laws and regulations embodying it. This is what many Americans sought to do with Senator Kerry's Section 907 of the Freedom Support Act that barred Azerbaijan from receiving any government-to-government support. Over many years those opposed to Section 907 struggled to change the Act but failed. In such cases, the only path forward is to accept the original legislation but seek to alter its implementation in such a way as to remove or at least minimize the problem. This is what opponents of 907 finally resigned themselves to doing. Thanks to a waiver process, they have been able successfully to mobilize supporters and sidestep what they considered the worst features of 907 through the issuance of annual waivers by the Under Secretary of State for Political Affairs. However, the original legislation remains a thorn in American-Azerbaijani relations.

The clear lesson to be drawn from this example is that it is usually futile to seek to rectify problems that trace to provisions of the Freedom Support Act or to analogous legislation in Europe by amending the original law or decree. The only practical way to correct problems that trace to original legislation is to do so through administrative measures that can be defended as being somehow consistent with the legislators' intent.

The second group of problems or shortcomings of Western policy in the Caucasus and Central Asia are those that arise from the organizational predispositions and habits of the governmental agencies to which legislators entrusted the implementation of their laws and decrees. In many cases, if not most, the resulting bureaucratic procedures lead to nightmarish complications that baffle and bother those trying to make a given program work. But in defense of the implementing agencies, it must also be acknowledged that many of their most negative practices arise from the endless constraints imposed on them by formal legislation or by the comments of members of Congress during hearings. With full justification, the bureaucrats will point to budget cycles imposed by Congress or by the European Council, Parliament, or European Commission, to the forms and timetables for reporting, and to detailed rules governing everything from procurement to accounting that constrain them. The purpose of all this oversight is to limit the extent and range of administrative caprice. Yet in practice it contributes to a bureaucratic formalism that stifles even the most responsible efforts to interpret the laws and regulations in light of realities on the ground. Worse, it is often used to justify inflexible and wooden practices that neutralize the legislators' intent.

It is never a simple matter to change the habits of administrative agencies, and Washington and Brussels are no exceptions. Nonetheless, it is possible to do so, making it the easiest and quickest way to effect changes in overall policy. Let us consider five specific areas in which problems of U.S. and European policy toward the Caucasus and Central Asia trace directly to structural issues or administrative practices that can be easily identified and rectified.

COORDINATE THE 'THREE BASKETS'

On no issue is bureaucratic formalism more dramatically on display, and with more nearly fatal consequences, than in the coordination among the various arms of the West's overall strategy for Central Asia and the Caucasus. We have already seen how that strategy came to be divided into three branches or "baskets," and have traced the origins of that tri-partite approach to a curious aspect of the 1975 Helsinki Final Act. To reiterate, the unstated goal of the negotiators at Helsinki was not to create a single and well-integrated structure of policy and practice but to separate the three realms from each other in such a way that progress could be made in one while one or more of the others was stalemated.. The Russians wanted trade and investment while the West wanted to control nuclear arms and advance the cause of human rights. For different reasons, both sides were glad to disaggregate the policy and seek gains in one or two areas, but not necessarily all three at once. The only real integration between the three occurred in the realm of some vague faith in the future, and not in the structure of the agreement itself.

It was therefore quite natural for the three baskets to be relegated to the care of institutionally separate bureaucracies: military, economic, and political/normative. It was also quite convenient, for neither in the East nor West were these bureaucracies at all accustomed to interacting with each other. To be sure, the Helsinki agreement also contained ten high-sounding principles ("the "Decalogue") governing the behavior of States towards their citizens, as well as towards each other, but these remained a dead letter. In Washington, it became customary to refer to the three baskets as separate "stovepipes" that functioned with little or no cooperation, let alone integration, among them . This institutional structure and the cast of mind that supported it thrived between the signing of the Helsinki Final Act in August 1975 and December, 1994, at which time it was transfigured with little or no change into the Organization for Security and Cooperation in Europe (OSCE).

The near-total absence of coordination between the three components or "stovepipes" continued as Europe and America launched their strategies for dealing with the new states formed after the collapse of the USSR. Whether or not this served the actual interests of the West, it was convenient to continue as before, and no one in either Washington or Brussels suggested any need for change. Security remained the exclusive responsibility of the Department of Defense, economic assistance fell to the Departments of State and Commerce, and democracy and human rights continued, as it had since 1977, under the Bureau of Democracy, Human Rights and Labor Affairs (DRL), a bureau within the State Department presided over by an Undersecretary of State for Civilian Security, Democracy, and Human Rights. Each reported separately to Congress, and indeed to different committees of Congress, and each remained subject to its own external interest groups, which included arms providers for DOD, western businesses and especially oil companies for Commerce, ethnic lobbies, and a well-institutionalized human rights lobby for DRL.

The great flaw in this arrangement is not that the bureaus were separate and remain so today. To some extent this is inevitable, given the sheer size of the enterprises involved. But no more senior official, presumably the Secretary of State or the National Security Advisor, accepted responsibility for coordinating them. In other words, America's failure to integrate its policy towards Central Asia and the Caucasus was *structural*, not philosophical. In Europe the problem was further exacerbated by the fact that the EU had no security arm and could therefore not have coordinated the three even if it had wanted to do so. *This meant that neither in Washington nor Brussels was there any serious capacity to negotiate relationships as a whole, nor does such a capacity exist today.* As a result, the West has systematically forgone most of the trade-offs and potential gains that might have been achieved through patient negotiation and deal-making with regional states.

Worse, as noted earlier, a single office – that of the Under Secretary of State for Civilian Security, Democracy, and Human Rights – has at times been able unilaterally to veto initiatives in the other two areas. Again, the issue is not whether democracy and rights are important, but whether relations in the other two areas should be completely suspended, as has happened with some frequency, until such a time that a given country reaches some threshold in this sphere. The issue is whether so primitive an approach – all sticks and no carrots – is effective in bringing about progress in *any* of the three realms. The record of the first quarter century of relations provides dramatic evidence that it is not. The solution is for a senior official to accept responsibility for the interagency process and thereby *bring about coordination.*

Bureaucratic Stove-Piping within the Regions and Between Them

Like it or not, bureaucratic structures deeply affect policy and its implementation. For most of the first quarter century of western relations with the countries of the Caucasus and Central Asia the relative isolation of U.S. embassies in both regions proved a handicap. Even though the common genealogy of the countries involved created common concerns, ambassadors and embassy staff in similar positions rarely met, and with predictable consequences. Inter-embassy contact and consultation has recently improved at the ambassadorial level but not at the level of embassy staffs. This must be corrected.

A more serious problem arises from the isolation from one another of regional bureaus within the Department of State. Down to 2008 all five former Soviet states of Central Asia fell under the Bureau of European Affairs. Since Russia fell under the same bureau, in practice this meant that the concerns of U.S. policy in these countries were often subordinated to those involving Russia. This arrangement also precluded discussion and co-ordination of U.S. policy in Central Asia and Afghanistan, which fell under a different Bureau. This self-defeating practice persisted for nearly a decade, during which Afghanistan was the U.S.' principal regional concern, and in spite of the fact that all involved realized that improvements in Afghanistan required cooperation between that country and its northern neighbors.

The establishment of a new Bureau of South and Central Asian Affairs in 2008 helped address this problem but at the price of isolating U.S. policy in Central Asia from what in fact are closely related concerns in the Caucasus. The Caucasus remained as it had always been, under the Bureau of European and Eurasian Affairs. While this arrangement makes sense, it carries two prices: first, that the three countries can easily become lost in a large bureau comprising more than three dozen countries and the EU, and, second, that it effectively isolates the Caucasus from Central Asia.

The importance of this point is growing daily. As long as the Caucasus was seen mainly as a corridor for exporting gas and oil westward to Europe the old arrangement was fine. But as it became clear that the main new east-west continental land corridors connecting China and India to Europe will pass directly through both Central Asia and the Caucasus, their relegation to two separate Bureaus within State has become an issue. Through a simple announcement backed by military will, Russia can close down east-west trade across either the Black Sea or Caspian or both. Besides the potential damage to Europe or China, such a move would give Russia effective control over both the Caucasus and Central Asia. Their most essential corridor of trade and interaction with both Europe and Asia would henceforth function only when Moscow permits it to. It therefore is important for the U.S. State Department and other agencies to be able easily to coordinate their policies and actions in both regions.

A further area in which greater communication is urgently needed is between the EU and U.S. In spite of fairly regular communication at upper levels, and in spite of considerable contact among embassies at the national level, coordination remains quite inadequate. As a result, there are many duplicating and overlapping programs. Besides increasing costs and decreasing effectiveness, such overlapping sows confusion within all the regional governments, which are placed in the position of coordinating U.S. and EU programs which those two major powers failed to coordinate on their own. The energy field provides an important example of this. America and Europe were relatively coordinated in their support for the Baku-Tbilisi-Ceyhan pipeline, though the U.S. did the lion share of the work. Yet as Europe grew more active in pursuing energy diversification after the 2006 Russian-Ukrainian energy war, it would have appeared logical for America and Europe to coordinate their efforts. Both promoted pipelines to export Turkmen natural gas – only they were different projects. Because of its focus on Afghanistan, Washington promoted the TAPI project, whereas the EU rediscovered the Trans-Caspian pipeline project supported by Washington in the 1990s. The lack of coordination ended up weakening both projects' chances of success.

A final and especially important area in which much greater coordination is called for is between both the US, EU and NATO. All three seek to advance a common strategy in the region, or should be doing so. But by their lack of coordination, they manage only to convince regional states that the West is not a reliable partner in the sphere of security. Several governments in Central Asia and the Caucasus do not believe that they can rely on the West to provide the third leg of the *strategic balance* between China, Russia, and the West that is the basis of their strategic concept. This is quite separate from the constant ebb and flow of security support provided by NATO. Here again the failure to maximize this on the level of both strategy and tactics can be blamed on inadequate communication and coordination in the West. As argued throughout this paper, this single most serious flaw in western strategy is a near-total lack of coordination among its various elements. Until such coordination exists, little of the "deal making" described above will be possible and even less will be effective.

No administrative borders inscribed on a map will resolve all problems of coordinating U.S. policies and programs in the Caucasus and Central Asia. But the institution of more regular contact among embassy staffs on a regional basis within the Caucasus and within Central Asia, and between key U.S. personnel in the Caucasus and Central Asia as a single region, will go far towards improving region-wide effectiveness. Further, regular contact between all U.S. and EU agencies operating in the Caucasus and Central Asia will bring immediate benefits both to the West and to the regional countries themselves. Finally, and particularly important, is to bring about greater contact and coordination between NATO, the U.S. and EU, so as to facilitate the trade-offs and "deal making" that is one of the main recommendations of this study.

COMPREHENSIVE NEGOTIATIONS TO IDENTIFY SYNERGIES

The parceling out of western concerns into three baskets has had the inevitable effect of treating them as separate variables rather than as inter-related components of a single program and strategy. This has caused the U.S. and EU to undervalue the importance of high level negotiations focusing on the interrelations among the three baskets and has allowed them to transform such negotiations into more narrowly bureaucratic affairs. While it is true that Assistant Secretaries of State meet from time to time with national leaders in the Caucasus and Central Asia, and that such meetings have sometimes yielded positive benefits for both partners, they are rarely, if ever, true negotiations spanning the full range of the relationship. Too often, partner countries perceive such meetings as a presentation of current American complaints, followed by the U.S. side presenting new projects to be embraced or rejected by the local partner. One national leader in the region characterized his meetings with top American diplomats as "a time when Washington administers grade-school scoldings and then lays out whatever new initiatives it is currently promoting, sort of like a bazaar."

Whatever U.S. or European diplomats may think of them, these sessions cannot be considered true negotiations and deal-making sessions based on the long-term interests of both parties. Rather than seek to match their priorities with ours and then come to agreements involving trade-offs on both sides, they tend instead to result merely in the affirmation of the lowest common denominator of interests. A similar process takes place between the EU and regional governments, although the existence of a single EU Special Representative to each *region* has, in recent years, resulted in more successful negotiations between the EU and regional governments.

To a large extent, this is due to the fact that the first concern of *all* regional states is with the preservation of their sovereignty and the security needs that they consider essential to that end. A more candid recognition of this reality on the part of the West will in itself open neglected possibilities in the area of trade-offs and *quid pro quos* involving economic relations, as well as political reforms and human rights. Since the EU has no military wing, this will be more difficult for the EU than for the U.S., but the involvement of EU countries in NATO should allow even the EU to engage with security issues more actively than it has to until now.

How, then, can this flaw, this "birth defect," of western strategy in the Caucasus and Central Asia, be rectified? In Washington, the answer lies squarely at the level of the National Security Council and especially the Secretary of State. The Secretary, working in coordination with the NSC and with the secretaries of Defense and Commerce, must assume responsibility for coordinating and integrating activities *in all three baskets*. The implementation can then be delegated to the Assistant Secretaries responsible for the Caucasus and Central Asia, but only with a high degree of oversight by the office of the Secretary.

Only in this way will the U.S. government be able to carry out its task in a manner that advances U.S. interests *in all three spheres together*, and not simply in those areas managed by State and ill-coordinated with the others. Such a process will actively foster coordination and integration among all three stovepipes. The challenge for the Secretary of State and colleagues in Defense and Commerce is to discern and build upon positive synergies among the three spheres; having done so, they must negotiate understandings and deals with partner countries that involve trade-offs which regional governments find useful for their own strategies, even as those trade-offs and deals support American ends.

Such an approach cannot succeed without a high-level, constant and more active interagency process than now exists. This consultative process must be continuous.

As part of this interagency process, when departments responsible for each of the three "baskets" report to Congress, they must include information on U.S. strategy as a whole, setting their own agency's activities in that larger, unitary framework. By so doing, they will communicate both the achievements and the trade-offs involved, and explain their agency's actions in terms of that larger strategy.

The kind of periodic high-level and meetings and agreements proposed here require careful preparation on both sides. To be effective, all involved must be conscious of the state of the relationship in all three "baskets" and must present American or European policy as a single whole and not simply the sum of three baskets. By identifying and promoting synergies across all three baskets, western ambassadors and other officials will more effectively ferret out possible synergies, which can then be fed into the higher-level discussions. Such negotiations will in turn inform the regional meetings that the EU has held with regional states since 2013, and which the U.S. launched in 2016 with its new Central Asia Five Plus One (C5 Plus 1) format. In the Caucasus, for obvious reasons relating to the Armenia-Azerbaijan conflict, such regional meetings do not exist, but that should not prevent American and European officials from coordinating their policies.

To summarize, in both bilateral and multilateral contexts the U.S. and EU should focus much more seriously on the relationships as a whole, identifying trade-offs and synergies between "baskets" and engaging their regional partners in a more comprehensive dialogue than exists today. Rather than frame the discussion as a choice between security, economic reform, and democracy and human rights, both sides should approach it as a negotiation involving delicate and evolving balances between them.

MOVING BEYOND "NAMING AND SHAMING"

No aspect of U.S. and European relations with Central Asia and the Caucasus has aroused more ardent support and at the same time more intense criticism that the annual reports from the Bureau of Democracy, Human Rights and Labor (DRL), and the Commission on International Religious Freedom (USCIRF).

To supporters, these compendia expose abuses in both spheres that might otherwise go unnoticed and provide a ready guide for targeting future campaigns and initiatives. To critics, the practice of "naming and shaming" causes regional governments to lose face in ways that are unproductive, and leads to breakdowns in the very relations that are needed to solve the problems thus identified. In other words, while both sides agree that they lead to adversarial relationships, one side defends such confrontations as a reflection of reality and the other sees them as a barrier to improvements.

Curiously, both friends and foes of these reports on basic rights agree that they are precisely what Congress had in mind in 1961 when it passed the Foreign Assistance Act. That legislation indeed calls for an enumeration of violations in both areas. What it notably fails to do is require the Department of State also to identify and report on initiatives and programs advanced by the United States to improve these situations, and positive steps, if any, that the regional government has taken on its own. On this basis, the State Department has focused overwhelmingly on the negative.

This study finds these reports useful and potentially beneficial, provided they are carefully researched, documented, and subjected to rigorous tests for accuracy. The question of accuracy will be examined shortly.

For now, let us note how the reporting might be deepened and thereby improved. What is needed is for Congress to receive reports on positive steps taken by the Department of State and other official U.S. bodies to find solutions to each problem enumerated. Such reporting should cover both the initiatives themselves and their effectiveness.

In other words, the reports should enable Congress not only to identify problems but to answer the question "What, if anything, is the U.S. doing to resolve the problem, and how effective have those efforts been?" This addition to the State Department's annual reporting does not require further legislation and can be initiated by the Department itself in order better to inform Congress.

Indeed, the Freedom Support Act already calls for "detailed explanation[s] of the assistance to be provided (including the dollar amounts of such assistance) and an explanation of how such assistance will directly benefit the needy people in such country." (sec. 161, p. 59). It is thus entirely consistent for the Department of State to add to its reports on Democracy and Human Rights and on Religious Freedom sections covering what specific steps the U.S. has taken to address each issue or group of issues cited. The Department of State should also introduce a longer time horizon into its reports, so as to indicate whether the overall trajectory of a given country is positive or negative.

STRENGTHENING GOVERNMENTS' IN-HOUSE ANALYTICAL CAPACITY

It is entirely appropriate for non-governmental organizations to collect information on the state of human rights and religious freedom worldwide and to share it with whomever they wish, including the U.S. government and the EU. What is neither appropriate nor acceptable is for the Department of State and European organs to accept uncritically such information, without subjecting it to the normal standards for evidence, and to use reports provided by others as an excuse for not gathering such information themselves. Yet this is just what has happened for twenty-five years in the Caucasus and Central Asia. Staff members at the State Department who assemble the annual reports on human rights, democracy, and religious freedom, not to speak of USCIRF, are hard-working and diligent but their numbers and resources are so limited that they feel they have no choice but to accept at face value many claims coming to them "over the transom." In other words, the Department of State has regularly provided Congress with claims lacking corroborating evidence and charges that it has not itself verified. This is inexcusable under any circumstances but even less so when it is known that the organization compiling the information is funded by groups like the Open Society Foundation which, as recent information leaks have confirmed, have a clear and highly political agenda.

This has led to some astonishing lapses, which should be blamed not just on the lobby groups that compiled the information but on the State

Department for uncritically accepting it. One case out of many that gained notoriety arose when a human rights activist in Uzbekistan, Andrei Shelkovenko, died on May 19, 2004, while in police custody. Human Rights Watch immediately issued a statement attributing the death to torture. This allegation was disseminated widely in the international press. At the suggestion of the Tashkent representative of Freedom House, the Uzbek Ministry of Internal Affairs convened an authoritative international investigative team to explore the validity of this claim. Membership in the group included several former U.S. ambassadors and the Chief Forensic Pathologist of the Province of Ontario. After an exhaustive investigation, which included an examination of Shelkovenko's body and family history, the investigative group concluded 1) that he did not die under torture; 2) that there was no evidence of his having been tortured; 3) that his death was a suicide through hanging, and 4) that Shelkovenko had a history of prior suicide attempts. But by then the damage had been done and the U.S. Government and EU, by injudiciously accepting Human Rights Watch's earlier claims, had greatly damaged their own credibility.

To correct this long-standing problem, all information on these issues which the State Department reports to Congress must henceforth be accompanied by credible evidence and reliable sourcing. If the State Department does not institute this change on its own, the Subcommittee on State, Foreign Operations, and Related Programs under the House Appropriations Committee should demand it through its annual request to the State Department.

CONCLUSIONS

These, then, are five areas in which U.S. and European policy is hindered not by conceptual problems or objective circumstances on the ground, but by structural and institutional practices that have been generated and perpetuated within western governments themselves. Since none are the results of legislative action, they can be addressed and corrected by the executive agencies themselves, without either amending or supplementing existing additional legislation.

The fundamental challenge is to overcome the mutual isolation of central bureaucracies from one another that was the legacy of the Helsinki accords. It is worth stressing the price the West is currently paying for *not* coordinating its various efforts and projects in Central Asia and the Caucasus. As noted above, this discourages the United States, European Union, and NATO from identifying and building upon the inter-relationships and trade-offs between the three baskets that potentially exist.

Not doing so, it prevents deal-making that could be equally beneficial to the West and to its regional partners. And it breeds confusion in the mind of the West's partners in the region as they struggle to make sense of uncoordinated western programs and policies.

Beyond these self-inflicted wounds, the uncoordinated nature of American and European policies in diverse fields condemns the West to pursuing a wooden and overly passive diplomacy that is not in its own interest or that of its regional partners. The West's failure to integrate its actions in diverse areas gives the impression that it is merely improvising, and not implementing any seriously conceived and deliberate strategy. The absence of integration in U.S. and European policy has undermined the widespread hope that sovereignty could be preserved and strengthened by balancing Russia with China and both of them with the West (US and EU) in a series of positive relationships. Stated simply, the West is not perceived as playing a serious role, or at least a role commensurate with what regional sovereignty, security, and peace require.

The emergence in 2016 of the U.S.-Central Asia "Central Asia Five Plus One" consultations vividly reflects this reality. As had been frequently noted over the years, the U.S. has much to gain from adding regular *regional* consultations to its program of existing bilateral ones. As of this writing, two meetings have been held and expectations for the future are high. However, the U.S.' response, as reflected in the agendas announced to date, is disappointing. Instead of grasping the potential benefits of such consultations for all parties, Washington has approached the agenda in a mechanical fashion, without advancing any proposals that would move beyond the pallid status quo. The five partner governments have responded politely, but privately ask if it is the U.S. intention to treat the Central Asia Five Plus One simply as one more periodic chore with little potential value to Washington or the five regional states. It is not too late to correct such an impression and to use the new format more actively to advance U.S. and regional interests simultaneously.

ENDNOTES

1. For the most recent such waiver see Federal register, 20 June 2016, https://www.federalregister.gov/articles/2016/06/20/2016-14504/authority-to-waive-section-907-of-the-freedom-support-act
2. https://www.usaid.gov/ads/policy/faa, esp. 161.
3. "George Soros: The Hillary Democrats' Billionaire Puppetmaster?", *Investor's Business Daily*, August 15, 2016.
4. "HRW Acknowledges Erroneous Uzbek Torture Allegation", *Radio Liberty*, June 2, 2004. (http://www.rferl.org/a/1053088.html)
5. John C.K. Daly, *Rush to Judgment: Western Media and the 2005 Andijan Violence*, Silk Road Paper, Central Asia-Caucasus Institute, May 2016, p. 6.
6. Ann McMillan, "Interdependency-Not Integration", in Colin Mackerras & Michael Clarke, eds., *China, Xinjiang and Central Asia: History, Transition and Crossborder Interaction into the 21st Century*, 2009, pp. 105-106.
7. S. Frederick Starr, "A Partnership for Central Asia," *Foreign Affairs*, July-August, 2005.

UPDATING AND UPGRADING STRATEGIC ASSUMPTIONS AND PRACTICES

■

Some of the problems with western strategy in Central Asia and the Caucasus trace to decisions by the U.S. President and Congress or the European Commission and Parliament. We have taken the view that the work of amending or supplementing existing legislation is so time consuming and its likely result so unpredictable that it does not make sense to pursue this potential avenue for improvement. We have argued that the second source of problems with western policy in the region are the bureaucratic practices of the western governments themselves. These practices are deeply embedded in the lives of many bureaus and organizations and in many cases are carried out quite unconsciously by those involved. Nonetheless, once officials are made conscious of them, they can relatively easily change, provided they wish to do so. This being the case, we proposed various concrete structural and organizational measures that will result in more effective implementation of policy.

Let us now turn to the third source of problems of western policy, namely, strategic assumptions that suffuse and define both the original legislation and the complex processes of implementing it. Being assumptions rather than acknowledged constants, they are rarely, if ever, made explicit, let alone discussed. Because of this, it is the more difficult to change them. Change, after all, involves rearranging the mental furniture in which legislators and bureaucrats alike pass their days quite comfortably. Nevertheless, it is worth a try, and in that spirit the authors propose ten areas in which the core assumptions require rethinking.

THE PRIMACY OF SOVEREIGNTY AND SECURITY

The United States has been secure in its borders since 1815. With the creation of the European Union at Maastricht in 1993, European countries have felt so secure from external threats that they have cut back expenditures on defense to an absolute minimum, or less. No country in the Caucasus or Central Asia enjoys this luxury. Like new sovereignties everywhere, they naturally feel insecure, usually with good reason. Positioned between a half dozen nuclear powers and faced with constant revanchist pressures from Russia and economic pressures (and opportunities) from China, they have adopted a defensive mentality, with all that implies. Whether or not they acknowledge it publicly, the preservation of sovereignty and the protection of existing borders is their first strategic concern, the *sine qua non* for all others.

If it expects to advance its own overall objectives in these regions, the West must fully accept this reality. This means responsibly responding to local concerns over threats to their sovereignty through such programs as NATO's Partnership for Peace and through many bilateral initiatives. Some of these might be proposed by the countries themselves, in terms of training, interoperability, technological gear, etc; and, when warranted, the provision of defensive arms and equipment. No one can doubt that economic development, investments, trade, and economic development advance security as much as do arms, open political systems, responsive governments, and the provision of education, health, and basic services. But the West can no longer expect to finesse the subject of hard security, for it is at the very front of the minds of all its national partners across the region. Conversely, soft security can no longer be treated as a surrogate for hard security, or as an alternative to it. Whatever the form or scale of the resulting security arrangements—and they will doubtless vary greatly from country to country—a clear-headed focus on the hard realities of regional security in both the Caucasus and Central Asia will become the precondition to successful mutual activities in all other areas or "baskets."

This calls for different actions in the various countries. Georgia, which has made a clear strategic decision to align itself with the West, requires actions that are supportive of that choice. Bluntly, this means that NATO must move beyond setting up storage facilities there to a range of initiatives in the area of "hard" security. All of the other states seek, with varying degrees of success, to preserve their sovereignties and identities by maintaining positive, balanced, and active relations with all major external powers. Whether or not leaders in Europe and the United States choose to acknowledge it, both America and Europe figure centrally in the security strategies of all regional countries. The West should accept this fact, and recognize that building positive relations in both the Caucasus and Central Asia is not only valuable in itself but urgently important to the countries themselves. A conscious acknowledgment of this reality and embrace of policies that advance each country's security are the best hope for advancing other Western interests and programs.

One might object that Moscow will surely consider such security-related measures as a threat to itself, as potentially offensive as well as defensive. The U.S. must be prepared to counter this claim directly and vigorously. It must show that such measures, being purely defensive, are not against anyone, and are simply necessary steps to creating regional security *from within*. Russia, too, wants security and stability; but believes that the only way to assure it in both the Caucasus and Central Asia is *from without*, in other words, through Russian domination of security affairs at the expense of local sovereignties. At no time in the long history of the Caucasus and Central Asia has such security *from without* proven sustainable in the long run. Under present circumstances, which can be defined as post-colonial, security imposed from Russia, China, or some other combination of external forces is bound to lead to instability. This is the case in great part because Russia's quest for a sphere of privileged interests, to use former Russian President Dmitry Medvedev's term,[1] is based not primarily on attraction but on coercion. As such, Russian dominance depends on the vulnerability of the regional states; for Russia to be able to bring them into line they have to be weak, corrupt, and largely authoritarian – and thus unstable.

In claiming to foster regional security from within, the U.S. and Europe must be prepared to address candidly Russia's concerns but without sacrificing the sovereign interests of the Caucasus and Central Asia and without negotiating over the heads of the latter. This will mean coming to certain mutual understandings in the security sphere. But even these understandings should be entered into through negotiations, in which both sides share balanced self-restraints and through which, in the end, they bring into being what in the nineteenth century was called a "concert."

The rationale for support for regional sovereignties and security is not to oppose other external powers. Rather, it is to enable Central Asians and Caucasians to build their own security, to be legal subjects rather than objects to be moved on a chessboard; in short, to become masters of their own fate. To this end, the West must link its security commitments with advances in economics and civic institutions and rights. The identification of possible synergies and trade-offs between the three baskets is the principal task of western diplomacy and deal-making in both the Caucasus and Central Asia.

ASSISTANCE AS REWARD?

In earlier chapters of this study the authors suggested that even a cursory glance at the distribution by country of projects pursued by the U.S. and the E.U. in Central Asia and the Caucasus indicates that both consider assistance as a kind of reward for good behavior, especially in the area of democratization. Thus, Kyrgyzstan could close the U.S./NATO base at Manas, allow corruption to metastasize and become endemic even in the NGO sector, and sacrifice important areas of its sovereignty by joining Russia's Eurasian Union in exchange for open and secret payments- and still receive the highest per capita level of U.S. assistance funds in the region. The assumption is that claims of having moved towards democracy, or at least of having made gestures in that direction, overshadow all other strategic considerations, and that such progress should be rewarded under the principle "more for more."

Faced with such an "all or nothing" approach by the West, regional governments all too often respond by reaching out instead to less demanding major powers, e.g. Russia or China. Worse, they perceive that the West, by picking regional favorites on the basis of this one criterion, is in fact pitting regional states against each other and generally fostering an adversarial relationship between itself and regional governments. In short, the narrowly defined "progress-reward" approach to democratization ends up by undermining all other western interests in the region.

Many Americans, including prominent political figures, observing the setbacks and failures of their government's drive for democratization abroad, feel that Washington should get out of this business.[2] Citing John Quincy Adams' famous dictum that the United States does not go abroad "in search of monsters to destroy," they argue that America can be a well-wisher of democratization everywhere but not its main sponsor, judge, and jury. Others argue that progress towards democracy should not be rejected as a goal but simply ranked as one important element among many western strategic objectives in the Caucasus and Central Asia. We believe this makes sense. It is most unlikely that any government in Europe or America would publicly support a dramatic move away from recent practice. Nor is that necessary. The problem is not the West's support for democracy as such, but its absolutist focus on national elections as the sole measure of democratic development, and the hectoring way in which its criticism is presented.

A more practical and efficacious approach is to accept the existing political arrangements in each country as a given and to evaluate their progress or retrogression with respect to democracy according to local conditions and traditions, i.e., the starting point. Instead of asking "did this election meet international standards of free and fair elections," let us ask instead "Did this election mark progress or retreat in comparison with the preceding election?" And having done so, let the U.S. and Europe ask in each case how this factor relates to their other interests in the country in question and in the region as a whole.

PROMOTING GOOD GOVERNANCE

Most Americans and Europeans take for granted the existence of an adequate civil service and local officialdom. They assume at least a minimal level of competence and honesty from those charged with collecting taxes or the issuance of passports and other papers, as well as from local police, courts, health and human services offices, recruitment agencies for jobs in government or business, legal services, banks, university admissions offices, or the scores of bureaucratic offices that issue permits and licenses. The Soviet Union was notorious for its glaring shortcomings in precisely these areas, the infuriating inefficiency of agencies serving the public, and the near-universal corruption that pervaded them . With the partial exception of Georgians, no one in either Central Asia or the Caucasus can assume that any of these agencies work effectively or fairly today. To be sure, improvements have been in achieved in some countries in some areas, but the overall picture remains grim. The application of modern administrative practices and the new technologies that support them is partial and sporadic at best. This can be blamed in part on the high costs of training and equipment needed to revamp sclerotic bureaucracies. The rise of the private sector across the region may also be a factor, for it has attracted much of the top talent in the rising generation. But the fact that the West has largely neglected this important sphere has certainly not helped matters.

The resulting situation profoundly affects all western programs and practices in both the Caucasus and Central Asia. Its first victims are initiatives in support of free and fair elections and democratization. Most locals consider it absurd to dream of implanting electoral democracy on top of a civil service that is considered incompetent and corrupt. Similarly, the West's support for non-governmental organizations, like the rise of the private sector, draws yet more competent and civic minded young people to posts outside the government. As we have noted, many of the most high-minded NGOs operate in open opposition to the government, which gives rise to a fortress mentality and resistance to change in the very quarters where greater openness is required. The result is stalemate and frustration on both sides.

The Freedom Support Act of 1991 included a provision to advance what it called "Governance" (sec. 133). The intent was good, but the legislation spoke only of efforts to stamp out corruption. Even though the act has been amended annually since then, no subsequent provision mandates USAID or other agencies to get at the root causes of the problem of corruption, let alone to extend the effort into the many diverse offices of partner states that directly affect citizens and their welfare. In other words, U.S. legislation treats corruption as a problem that can be reduced or eliminated through anti-corruption campaigns as opposed to fundamental reforms designed to advance good governance.

The general indifference of the Freedom Support Act to effective and responsive administration was the natural by-product of its single-minded focus on democratization. Its drafters simply assumed that democratically elected bodies would cut back and magically transform the entire bureaucratic apparatus. In recent years there has grown up a valuable body of writing that seeks to identify the links between democracy, economic development, and security. Against those who are fond of citing India as proof that a poor country can also be democratic, scholars like Stephen D. Krasner of Stanford and Latin Americanist Merilee S. Grindle of Harvard have argued that "democracy" is not an independent variable, nor is a market economy.[3] Both require a solid base of what Grindle felicitously calls "good enough governance." In Grindle's judgment, this consists of three elements: 1) security, 2) better provision of services, and, 3) economic growth. Both Grindle and Krasner argue that without these three attributes, it is naïve and unrealistic to think of building democracy. In short, "Good enough governance" is the necessary and unavoidable precondition for democratization.

We have noted how both the U.S. and EU have supported non-governmental organizations as instruments for fostering democratization in their countries. A consequence of this approach is that neither the U.S. nor EU have devoted major attention to the existing political leaders and elites who are inevitably involved with any institutional change or introduction of new practices. These are viewed instead as inevitable impediments to reform who must be brought into line through external pressure and coercion. Krasner addresses this problem directly, and offers a starkly different perspective. While sympathetic to the often heroic citizens who champion democratic reform, he argues that: "despite the potential for corruption, the support or endorsement of local political elites is a necessary condition for success [in democratization]. Without such support, external actors will fail in their efforts to improve local governance ...They must therefore focus on modest objectives that include the preferences of the national elites."[4]

As we have argued repeatedly on these pages, this means working *with* local governments rather than *on* them. But Krasner goes further. Having demonstrated the link between good governance and democratization, he then proceeds to show the ways in which security affects both good governance and democratization: "The first goal of 'good enough governance' must be to provide some level of security. Without a minimal level of security, economic growth and the provision of many services will be impossible." And while 'greater prosperity' does not guarantee consolidated democracy, it does make it more likely.[5]

The experience of Central Asia and the Caucasus is entirely consistent with these conclusions. To repeat, democratization is not an independent variable, and Grindle's "good enough governance" is indeed needed to provide the security and economic growth that facilitate democratization and are preconditions to it. If this is true, and no one has yet presented a serious counter-argument, it has the most serious implications for western programs in the region. Bluntly, to focus on elections and democratic processes without first attending to the essential support institutions is to attempt to build a house from the roof down. Not surprisingly, it has largely failed.

In spite of the Freedom Support Act's silence on good governance as a strategic goal, U.S. agencies have a clear Congressional mandate to address the over-arching problem of administrative reform in the states of Central Asia and the Caucasus. Under the rubric of "facilitating reform" a host of sections added after 1992 open the door to this. Additional later sections that speak of "support for transition" have also been interpreted to permit U.S. agencies to direct skills and resources to what we are calling "good governance." Similarly, both the EU and individual European countries that offer development assistance to the Caucasus and Central Asia have ample legislative mandate for the same activity. Finland, for example, which devoted many years to reforming the management of the National Bank of Kyrgyzstan, is just one example among many of such activity. Thus, the problem is not that the U.S. or EU are unable to address governance issues, or that they have failed to do so, but that their efforts have been too limited in scale and are not defined in terms of the kind of good governance that most directly affects citizens welfare and outlook.

The single most striking achievement in the area of "good governance" instituted by any government in the Caucasus or Central Asia since the collapse of the USSR are the Justice Houses established by the Saakashvili government in Georgia following the Rose revolution of November 2003. These institutions, which today exist in all the principal cities of Georgia, bring together in one place representatives of all the major governmental offices serving citizens' needs and with which citizens have reason to interact with some frequency. This convenient arrangement, which is facilitated by modern technologies linking the Justice Houses with all the governmental agencies represented there, enables a Georgian to get a passport, register a title to a car or house, pay taxes, or conduct many other transactions quickly and efficiently, through a kind of "one stop shopping." It is a remarkable innovation that can readily be adopted elsewhere. Indeed, Azerbaijan's ASAN centers follow essentially the same principle. But it should be noted that Georgia's Justice Houses – not to speak of Azerbaijan's ASAN centers – were established and operate without any direct support either from the U.S. or EU. To put it mildly, it is paradoxical that what is arguably the most significance advance in open and honest state-citizen relations anywhere in recent years was carried out in a country where the West claims to be fostering "democracy," but without either western money or expertise.

Thus, western countries should henceforth focus far more attention than formerly on reforms and training programs that lead to "good governance" in all areas affecting the lives of citizens on the ground that this is in itself beneficial and also because it is a necessary prerequisite for any future improvements in the sphere of democratization.

A critic might reasonably object that this approach accepts and even protects authoritarian rule, which the West should instead staunchly oppose. Such a critic might also point out that authoritarian rulers are masters at finding security threats everywhere and using them to protect their rule. This is true. But authoritarianism has deeper causes as well, not least in the deep political culture of peoples. This is why authoritarian regimes, as often as not, are replaced not by democracies but by other authoritarian regimes. If the preconditions have not been built, no imposed democracy can be sustainable. Such realities lend support to the approach set forth above, as opposed to treating public shows of "democracy" as facts that demand immediate rewards from the West.

WORKING *WITH* GOVERNMENTS, NOT *ON* THEM

The idea of promoting good governance as a precondition of further reforms seems so obvious that one may well ask why it has not been implemented more fully before now. The answer is equally obvious: too often, the West has considered institutions in Central Asia and the Caucasus that were inherited from the Soviet era as unwelcome holdovers from the past. On the quite reasonable assumption that they were populated by bureaucrats with unreconstructed Soviet mentalities, they have treated them as the enemy, to be avoided at all cost. Change, they assumed, would come about not through direct engagement but through the activities of young and modern men and women working outside the government in NGOs.

We will shortly focus directly on NGOs in these regions. Many have succeeded in bringing about positive change by fostering good governance, especially in such fields as public health, the recruitment and advancement of women, and the defense of legal rights. They have generally avoided collaborations with government agencies in part from the fear that they might be drawn into the corruption that prevails in many official bodies. But in the end, their effectiveness has been severely limited by the fact that their work often threatens local administrators and elites and throws them on the defensive. Notwithstanding good intentions, the NGOs have stalemated reform as much as they have fostered it. This is because, as Krasner insists, the endorsement of local elites is necessary for successful democratization.

The only recourse, then, is to work *with* local officials and administrators rather than *on* them. This need not lead to a general rejection of non-governmental organizations as instruments for promoting good governance. However, it requires shifting the balance in favor of work with official bodies. The European Union's Eastern Partnership (EaP) has done just this, and can cite advances in many countries. But among the countries of the region, only Armenia, Azerbaijan and Georgia participate in the EaP, and to wildly differing degrees. Can the same approach work in the less westernized societies of Central Asia? The experience of a Slovenian NGO activist and former staffer at Freedom House in New York, Mjusa Sever, provides stunning evidence that it can. Sever, who had recently founded Regional Dialogue, an NGO, entered into an agreement with Uzbekistan's Ministry of Justice to provide training in modern western criminal court procedure for Uzbek criminal defense attorneys. Regional Dialogue then opened direct contacts between the Ministry of justice and leading American lawyers and judges. John R. Tunheim, who now serves as the Chief U.S. District Judge in the District of Minnesota, made twelve trips to Uzbekistan over seven years in connection with this activity. And criminal defense attorney Mark Schamel of the law firm Womble Carlyle Sandridge and Rice made trips there for the same purpose. A typical seminar organized for the visiting Americans would focus not on abstract theory but on practical skills needed for a criminal defense lawyer, including the cross examination of witnesses, etc. Mr. Schamel reports that his seminars were attended by equal numbers of criminal defense attorneys, prosecutors, and judges, drawn both from Tashkent and other parts of the country. Reciprocating these teaching visits, Uzbek criminal defense attorneys made four visits to the U.S., during which they studied court procedures, the work of criminal defense attorneys, and law firms in Boston, Minnesota, and the District of Columbia. Finally, it should be noted that, thanks also to Regional Dialogue, the Chief Pathologist of the Government of Uzbekistan spent six months in the United States studying the work of professional colleagues there.

This experience testifies eloquently to the possibility of working *with* regional governments and their officials rather than *on* them. The European Union's Rule of Law Initiative provides countless other examples. These can and should be replicated many times over, and in all those fields that are considered essential to the interaction of citizens and their government, and to the cause of good governance and democratization.

Working with rather than on local governments in areas pertinent to civic welfare is not only possible but essential. By replacing a conflictual model of interaction between western donors and local governments with a collaborative one, this approach has already proven its worth. And as so often happens, success breeds success, and in the process overcomes mutual suspicion.

REDUCING RELIANCE ON NGOS

We have argued that the U.S. and EU should reduce their one-sided reliance on NGOs as instruments of change and shift the focus more in the direction of interaction with official bodies. This proposition requires further explication, for it is by no means obvious to many people of good will and progressive thinking in both Europe and America and flies directly in the face of much current policy.

The West's embrace of NGOs as instruments for change in countries abroad is quite recent, dating to the independent groups that appeared in Poland and Czechoslovakia and began challenging many practices of the Communist 1970s, when Solidarity in Poland and Charter 77 in Czechoslovakia boldly established autonomous organizations that challenged state policies in many realms, including labor and culture. The so-called Jazz Section in both countries succeeded in obtaining a charter from the United Nations and used that cover to publish banned books and convene discussions on sensitive topics.

The collapse of the USSR occurred just as this movement, by then supported by several American foundations, reached its apogee. The term "civil society," which formerly had been applied to a society as a whole that existed under law and extended to all the right to organize independently, now came to apply only to the "independent sector," i.e., the NGOs. As it became clear that the successor states had inherited from the USSR many structures and habits deemed incompatible with the new freedoms, those who had supported "civil society" before the breakup now championed NGOs as the best agents for change in post-Soviet societies. Western governments, including the U.S. and EU, lent generous financial support to such groups.

In spite of gains NGOs brought about in several spheres, many of them fell prey to predictable pathologies. They were by no means immune to the widespread corruption around them. Worse, because their main and often sole funding came mainly or exclusively from abroad, they lacked the deep local roots that local giving and voluntarism had developed in America and which earned the admiration of the French politician and writer Alexis de Tocqueville. This has given their domestic critics ample grounds for arguing that they are not voluntaristic and that they are non-governmental only in the host country, while living meanwhile off grants from foreign governments.

In societies where institutions of all sorts had fallen prey to corruption under Soviet rule, it was probably inevitable that the post-independence NGOs funded by western governments would also feel the corroding disease of corruption. This indeed happened. With access to western money, a class of local NGO managers grew up. Experienced in grant writing (often thanks to western-sponsored classes in grantsmanship) , they knew how to cast proposals in such a way as to appeal to western donors. As western grants rose and fell, they learned how to move deftly from project to project, bringing their corrupt practices with them. So numerous are reported instances of corruption in this sphere that it is perhaps unfair to single out any one case. So let the following instance stand for many. When the government of Finland sponsored a Kyrgyz group dedicated to advancing women's empowerment it reasonably expected that such an organization actually existed. But when an official visiting from Helsinki attempted to visit the group's office, it found instead only a modern and well-appointed apartment, which turned out to be the sole "product" of Finnish largesse. Adroitly written reports had completely masked the corruption. Such instances of malfeasance may be exceptional, but their existence undercut the legitimacy of the NGO sector in both the Caucasus and Central Asia.

A more serious problem is that far too many independent groups and their western sponsors adopted an adversarial relationship with government officials, who amply reciprocated the hostility. Because it was governments that had to change, NGOs' considered it their task to cajole or embarrass them into doing so. Many decent government officials viewed the non-governmental initiatives in an entirely different light. They faced daily the extraordinary stresses generated by the rapid imposition of new governmental structures, laws, and property relations. They appreciated the actual weakness of the new states, and the internal and external threats to their independence and viability. Far from seeing NGOs as independent, they viewed them instead as agents of foreign governments and centrifugal forces in new national societies that were desperately in need of centripetal forces to bind them together. Over time it became a stand-off, with each side loudly proclaiming the latest iniquity perpetrated by the other, and invoking national or international public opinion in its defense. Following the model of Putin's Russia, pressures to register, regulate, and eventually ban foreign-funded NGOs rose throughout the region.

Deep skepticism about NGOs has arisen not only from authoritarian rulers like Putin but from modern-thinking and pro-democratic officials like Ashraf Ghani, a former World Bank official and, since 2014, President of Afghanistan. While serving as his country's Minister of Finance in 2002, Ghani argued before the 2002 Tokyo Donors' Conference that by providing support directly to NGOs, without coordinating with the government or even informing it, donors damaged the necessary links between citizens and the state and hence weakened the government. He concluded that support that completely bypasses governments does more harm than good.

As this situation developed, the West's embrace of NGOs as its principal local agents of change came under increasing criticism within Europe and America. Skeptics included American political scientist Nelson Kasfir who, even before Ghani's speech, published a penetrating essay criticizing the "conventional Notion" of civil society.[6] Critics arose from developing countries as well, as for instance the points raised by the Zapatista movement in Mexico and described by A.C. Dinerstein in his study *The Snail and the Good Government*.[7]

This is not the place to review this large and growing literature. But one thing is clear. As English geographer Claire Mercer put it in a review of the literature, "One of the most striking features of the anglophone literature on NGOs is the diversity of NGO sectors and their contributions to civil society and democracy; yet, exploration of this complexity is often eschewed in favor of a normative approach in which the apparently mutually enhancing relationship between NGOs, civil society and the state is underpinned by liberal democratic assumption rather than an engagement with wider debates about the politics of development."[8]

Mercer instead proposes "a more contextualized and less value-laden approach to the understanding of the political role of NGOs." Any assessment of the NGO sector and "civil society" in Central Asia and the Caucasus that is carried out in such a spirit is bound to reach a more nuanced conclusion than what is embodied in current U.S. and EU practice.

Thus, the U.S. and EU must severely cut back their current reliance on "civil society" and one-sided support for NGOs as the chief instruments of positive change in Central Asia and the Caucasus. Those NGOs that continue to receive support should be strongly encouraged to identify common interests with relevant governmental agencies and to develop constructive collaborations to further them. This should not and need not require any serious and honest NGO to abandon its commitments. Rather, it proposes a more efficacious and practical means of advancing them.

SUPPORT FOR SECULAR LAWS, GOVERNMENT, AND LEARNING

When the U.S. Congress developed the Freedom Support act in 1992 it affirmed and embraced the package of priorities and goals that underlay the 1975 Helsinki Agreements. The one change, and a very important one, was to add a clear statement on the importance of preserving and strengthening the new sovereignties and enhancing their security. Down to about 2010 officials repeated this affirmation whenever they were called upon to explain U.S. objectives in either the Caucasus or Central Asia. They interpreted this mandate broadly to include initiatives far beyond the area of security, and especially in the economic sphere. Thus, the U.S.' staunch commitment to the Baku-Tbilisi-Ceyhan pipeline, which was not led by American investors and does not send oil to American markets, was based on the solid principle that it would enhance the sovereignty and security of both Azerbaijan and Georgia, and also undergird Turkey's commitment to the security of its neighbors in the Caucasus.

With the one exception of affirming the central importance of the new states' sovereignty, the pillars of American and European strategy reflected commitments that had been repeated in numerous settings over many decades, to wit, support for democracy, human rights and religious freedom; free markets; trade and investment; and the security of both the U.S. and its partner countries. As the years passed, two further concerns forced themselves onto the attention of American and European lawmakers and administrators: to curtail drug trafficking to and through the regions, and to stamp out terrorism and the networks that perpetrate it, among them being radical Islamic movements. The U.S., EU, the OECD, and individual countries in Europe, as well as Canada, Japan, and Australia devoted substantial sums to these causes, with mixed results. They did so under the clear understanding that both constituted important (if heretofore neglected) dimensions of the goal of establishing and protecting security which they had already affirmed. Over the ensuing years these two "add ons" assumed ever greater importance in western activity in Central Asia and the Caucasus. Indeed, it became a commonplace to list them along with the promotion of democracy, rights, markets, and security as the West's strategic goals.

From the outset Western countries were concerned about the potential appeal of radical ideologies in the Muslim-majority areas of the former Soviet Union. In some quarters, this translated into an expectation of a competition between what was then the secular Turkish model and the Islamist Iranian theocratic model in the region. That neglected the fact that neither country had the resources to replace Russia as the dominant force in either the Caucasus or Central Asia; or that the Shi'a Iranian theocracy had little appeal to the Sunni populations of Central Asia.

The West fully acknowledged the urgent need to contend with religious extremism in all its dimensions. But the tactical measures it adopted to counteract it did nothing more than mechanically duplicate what the U.S., Europe and diverse international bodies were doing elsewhere. These focused more on the manifestations of extremism than its causes. Regarding the causes of extremism, a distinct paradigm developed in the late 1990s, which argues that repressive governments and economic deprivation are the main incubators of radicalism.[9]

But the paradigm, advanced primarily by the International Crisis Group, is disconnected from the general literature on radicalization. One scholar concludes that "none of the major theorists on radicalization suggest that there is a universal model with predictive certainty."[10] And among the many explanations advanced in the literature, repression does not have a prominent position. In fact, several overviews on the causes of radicalization hardly mention generalized repression at all, focusing only on discrimination against specific groups. One of the few systematic studies of the role of repression on radical Islamic movements, by Mohammed Hafez, concludes that the record is mixed. The policy recommendation of the dominant paradigm has been that instead of repressing political Islam, governments should open their political systems to competition; that would, in turn, deflate the balloon of radicalism that is being created by the repressive environment and the lack of avenues for opposition. Yet countries that have followed these recommendations have seen the opposite occur, as the examples of Pakistan and more recently Turkey indicate.

It is significant that those scholars and observers who warn of the counter-productive implications of repression in Central Asia tend not to be experts on radicalization, but observers of Central Asian politics and/or human rights activists. Their criticism is influenced by their general condemnation of the policies of Central Asian regimes, rather than the specifics of radical Islam. Criticism of policies in the field of religion is often part and parcel of a broader criticism of authoritarian and repressive policies and, moreover, is motivated by ethical considerations rather than political analysis. In other words, critics of repression often oppose it because they consider it wrong, not because of unassailable evidence that it foments extremism.

For Western policy, the implication of the paradigm was clear. The best way to curtail terrorism was to withdraw support from any regime judged to be repressive and to redouble investment in the "democracy agenda." Conveniently ignored was the fact that Kyrgyzstan, which could boast of being the most tolerant governments in Central Asia down to 2005, spawned many virulent strains of religious extremism, especially in its southern provinces, while Turkmenistan, which responded to religious activists with an iron fist, had few. Uzbekistan's uncompromising support for the officially recognized Muslim tradition, paired with a repressive approach to what were considered deviant strains of the faith, produced several outbursts of Islamic extremism down to about 2005 but these largely died out thereafter. And majority Shi'a Azerbaijan imposed a kind of firewall between religion and government, which has not led to widespread religious extremism or major acts of terrorism.

We do not offer these examples in support of any one theory of the causes of radical Islam or terrorism, but rather to point out that the region offers so many exceptions to the notion that repression gives rise to terrorism as to make it useless as a basis for policy. Much the same can be said of the line of thinking that traces terrorism to poverty. Like bad politics, poverty doubtless plays a role, but the fact remains that far more of the world's most dangerous terrorists arose from middle class and professional families than from the poor.

This is not the place to offer yet another thesis on the cause of radical Islamic movements. Rather, let us simply note that wherever they exist, they take as their goal the capture of the state, its resources, all the administrative agencies through which it carries out its will, and education. For all their differences in tactics, and for all the disagreements and conflicts that have arisen between such movements, they all agree that the object of their efforts is less the soul of individual believers than the instruments of state power. Communists dreamed of seizing the state in order to make it serve the proletariat: Islamists aspire to seize power in order to place it in the service of the faith and of themselves.

To now, the Western response to the rise of radical Islam has been twofold: fight the violent Islamist groups under the euphemisms of "War on Terror" and "Countering Violent Extremism", while *promoting* the notion of "Muslim Democrats." Without minimizing or denying the need for a military response to armed Islamist groups, it is unlikely that any military response can succeed in the absence of other measures that target the ideological movement underpinning the violent groups. Economic development and less capricious governance may also help, but have yet to provide the kind of vaccination against extremism and terrorism that their champions hoped for. Nor have initiatives outside the state turned the tide, as was noted above in the discussion of "civil society." Like it or not, the West's efforts to combat religious extremism must engage directly with the states themselves. Religious radicalism is directed above all toward the state, and any response must begin in that quarter, and not merely with negative measures.

As for Western positive measures, they have meant to provide a ground for the purveyors of deeply anti-Western ideologies, in the hope that they will moderate once repression is lifted. Everywhere in the Muslim world, Western leaders and thinkers have argued that if non-violent Islamist groups are allowed to operate in the political system, they will "moderate;" and that in any case, the old political Islam is being replaced by "Muslim Democrats", who appeal to conservative social values but are democratic politicians rather than Islamist ideologues.[12] The question where the predominant paradigm went wrong is beyond the scope of this study. But it should be mentioned that in a key article heralding the rise of "Muslim Democracy", the author focuses exclusively on the promise of new political parties, and does not mention the role of government institutions even once.[13] Yet where these "Muslim Democrats" have come to power, they have almost invariably turned out to return rapidly to their ideological roots, and to seek to consolidate and maximize power – at the expense of weakening those checks and balances and government institutions that existed. Turkey's AKP and the Egyptian Muslim Brotherhood are the two most obvious examples of this, and indicate that the Western support of "moderate Islamism" has been a distinct failure.

This is the point, finally, at which the interests of the West and of the news states of Central Asia and the Caucasus come into mutual alignment. To understand how this has come to be, let us note an important feature of their very otherwise very different histories.

The modern West addressed the problem of religious extremism in two very different phases. The first began with the Reformation and Counter-Reformism and culminated in the 1648 Peace of Westphalia. Convening in the German towns of Munster and Osnabruck, 109 delegations from diverse empires, states, and imperial cities agreed on the principle that whoever rules in a given territory has the power to name the religion under which its subjects live. Under the principle of *cujus regio, eijus religio* ("Whose realm, his religion") each state was sovereign and the head of each sovereign territory could name the religion to be followed there.

The second phase began with the English Revolution in 1647 and culminated in the "Glorious Revolution" of 1688, the American Bill of Rights introduced by James Madison on June 8, 1789, and the French Revolution. By very different routes, all three western countries, and after them most other major states of Europe, adopted not only the principle of religious toleration but, importantly, the separation of religious law from the law of the land.

America's decisive contribution to this important development was the First Amendment to its Constitution, which prohibits "the making of any law respecting an establishment of religion, or the free exercise thereof."

To be sure, some European countries continued to maintain an established church thereafter, but now under radically new conditions. Throughout the nineteenth and twentieth centuries the West in general accepted the fundamental principle that the state is secular in character and both the laws and the system of justice that serves them are to be secular.

Then a further basic element was added: beginning with the Scientific Revolution and extending through the establishment of the University of Berlin as a research institution in 1810, western countries came to embrace the freedom to teach and freedom to learn (*Lehrfreiheit und Lernfreiheit*). In other words, the West embraced the ideal of secularism in state-sponsored education.

So deeply are the principles of the secular state, secular systems of law, and secular education embedded in the Western consciousness that they are simply assumed, taken for granted. This, no doubt, is why it did not occur to the authors of the Freedom Support Act or any other major legislation affecting the new states formed after the collapse of the Soviet Union to include these principles among their strategic affirmations and goals. This was a serious mistake.

The Communist system that Moscow imposed on Central Asia and the Caucasus decisively secularized the state, law and the courts, and education. To this extent it was in step with broader developments in Europe and the North Atlantic region. However, in secularizing these functions, Soviet rulers proceeded to charge a new quasi-religious body—the Communist Party—with detailed supervision of the state, courts, and education. The Party carried out this assignment with unprecedented brutality and linked it closely with a general war against religion as such. The new states of the Caucasus and Central Asia inherited all this. They abolished the role of the Communist Party but to greater or lesser extent imposed the state itself in the space thus vacated.

This is the situation that exists today. By many steps both large and small the new states have endeavored to untangle the tight knot that had choked the law, courts, and education in Soviet times. The task is exceedingly complex and progress has been slow. Many mistakes have been made along the way, and there have been more than a few steps backwards, as Western critics have rightly noted. It is all a work in progress. Yet for the difficulties, the states of Central Asia and the Caucasus have achieved a distinctive and highly important status:

- They all have secular systems of governments. The legal status and degree of independence of religious bodies remains in flux, but the states themselves meet normal standards of secularism.
- Whatever the state of reform, they all have secular systems of law and secular courts. Even Afghanistan, which is officially called "The Islamic Republic of Afghanistan," has a legal system based on Roman law, not the Sharia.
- Their educational systems are all open to modern secular knowledge. Indeed, Central Asia and the Caucasus, with fewer than 100 million people (less than half the number of

Pakistan alone), have established more new and modern institutions of higher education than all their Muslim neighbors together.

It remains a mystery why Western powers have not embraced these achievements and the core western principles on which they are based as cornerstones of its strategy in Central Asia and the Caucasus. The reason appears to be that, accustomed to viewing the region through the lens of the USSR, the West has narrowly fixed its attention on areas that have yet to be reformed, not acknowledging the positive aspects of what does exist. Dramatically absent from this approach is any recognition of how profoundly significant the features listed above are when viewed in the context of neighboring Muslim societies, including Pakistan, Iran, Iraq, Turkey, and the rest of the Middle East.

In other words, those who persist in viewing the Caucasus and Central Asia solely through the lens of post-Soviet development are blind to the important place the region holds within the broader context of Muslim societies. Central Asia is not a remote outlier to the core regions of Islam but is itself a core region of the faith. Its religious leaders compiled nearly all of the most authoritative collections of the Sayings (Hadiths) of the Prophet Mohammad, and one of them, al-Bukhari from what is now Uzbekistan, was responsible for Islam's second most holy book after the Koran. Central Asian thinkers pioneered many, if not most, of the achievements generally attributed to medieval Arab scientists and philosophers. Azerbaijan, with its secular state, laws and education, is one of only four Shia-majority societies, and Iran's Azerbaijanis were historically responsible for the establishment of the state of Iran as a Shia polity in the first place.

The West, then, should view Central Asia and Azerbaijan as a largely successful and functioning laboratory for moderate Islam in the modern world. It should embrace the strengthening and improvement of secular states there as a strategic goal, and also the establishment of secular systems of law, courts, and educational institutions. Recognizing the ample shortcomings and deficiencies that exist, it should work patiently but tenaciously with governments and societies there to correct them. This strategic goal should be assigned the same level of importance as security, democratic development, the protection of rights and freedoms, and economic development. Indeed, the advancement of secular governance, courts, and education across these regions may prove not only to be the key to progress in the other strategic areas but the most lasting contribution the West can make in these historic lands of Islam.

IMPROVING ACCESS TO NEWS AND INFORMATION

North Atlantic leaders between 1945 and 1991 fully understood that Soviet officials considered news and information to be an essential component of their overall strategy for confronting the West. In response, both Europe and America devised large scale programs in radio, television, and print media that played a significant role in breaking the Soviet state's monopoly of information available to its citizens. With the collapse of the Soviet system, western governments concluded that these activities were no longer needed and closed down most of them. The rise of the Internet in the same years encouraged many to believe that citizens of the former USSR would soon be connected digitally to the entire world and that home computers and smartphones would obviate the need for special programs in the sphere of information.

For more than a decade it has been clear that these views were wrong, and that the need for western societies to reach out to the peoples of the USSR through diverse media, far from disappearing, was growing daily. Vladimir Putin's close attention to the world of information and the countless initiatives he has mounted in this sphere has expanded the need for a western response exponentially.

While Europeans and Americans are aware of Russia's RT television channel and its intensive feeding of stories to receptive western media, they are largely unaware of the extent to which Russian television, internet sources, and print media dominate the information space throughout the Caucasus and Central Asia. To be sure, Russia is not a monolith, and the views of at least a few independent Russians find their way into Russia's public media from time to time. But the channels of information that dominate the airwaves and print media of the Caucasus and Central Asia are those that reflect official views in Moscow rather than those of dissidents. China's Xinhua news agency is also very active across the region, thanks to news stories translated into local languages. Readily available to editors, these often find their way into print or form the basis of reports on television. As to western voices, with rare exceptions they are inaudible or inaccessible to all but a small number of local elites who know English or European languages.

In the absence of a more comprehensive media strategy by western countries, local audiences across the region, if they follow western sources at all, rely mainly on the British Broadcasting Company (BBC). BBC receives high marks from local listeners but its audience remains small, consisting mainly of elites. Voice of America and Radio Liberty continue to broadcast to both regions, but to diminished audiences. The reason for this is clear. Due to the lack of qualified linguists in the West, most of those reporting on American and European radios are *émigrés* from the region. While some of them are both talented and dedicated, many fall back on outdated clichés or produce poorly sourced accounts that strike their regional listeners as quaint or out of touch. Rather than blame the reporters for this, however, one should look to inadequate supervision and editing, and to decisions taken at higher levels in their organizations, including their supervisory boards, notably America's Broadcasting Board of Governors.

A number of studies have concluded that the U.S. government's foreign broadcasting network is failing at its task. A 2013 report of the Office of the U.S. Inspector General depicted an agency with a dedicated staff but with a governing board that is incompetent, useless and fatally broken. The report bluntly panned the foreign broadcasting agency as "dysfunctional" and "ineffectual."[14] Under the Broadcasting Board of Governors is the International Broadcasting Bureau (IBB), which "is responsible for the agency's strategic planning and oversight, including U.S. international media's innovation strategy, transmission, marketing, and program placement services for all BBG networks, including the Voice of America, Radio Free Europe/Radio Liberty."[15] Staffed in part by Foreign Service officers on two-year rotations, this body has adopted a bland and passive "business as usual" approach, which reflects the larger strategic failure. There is little or no evidence that anyone at higher levels of the State Department has ever addressed the many issues involved, let alone called for a comprehensive communications and information strategy that address the acute information crisis throughout Central Asia and the Caucasus.

Europe's Euronews channels has grown considerably since its creation in 1993. While it broadcasts in eleven languages, including Russian, Turkish and Persian, it is scarcely available in Central Asia and the Caucasus, and available nowhere in a local language.

Both the U.S. State Department and the European Commission should designate improving access of citizens of Central Asia and the Caucasus to Western news, information and communications as a major strategic priority, and should charge relevant boards and agencies to devise comprehensive plans to achieve that objective.

USING ONE YARDSTICK FOR ALL

The problem of different yardsticks is not a new problem. As far back as 1979, conservative critic and later UN Ambassador Jeane Kirkpatrick, in an essay and subsequent book entitled "Dictatorships and Double Standards," argued that standards were being applied to Egypt that would apply equally, if not more so, to many other states that were not coming under censure. In both works she argued against excessively pressuring rulers in such countries on the grounds that it was possible and even likely that they would be replaced by something worse. Then in 1985 Tom Kahn, in a speech before a conference organized by the left-wing Young Social Democrats (YSD), argued that no state should be written off on the basis of its past record, and the U.S. should promote evolutionary change even in authoritarian states. He noted that: "In contrast to the political democracies, which appeared on the scene only in the last two centuries, and in contrast to the totalitarian state, which appeared only in this century, many of the authoritarian societies are rooted in ancient social structures, while others are in transition to modern forms. Some display a bizarre blend of the modern and the archaic."[16]

Kahn's argument, like that of Kirkpatrick, bears directly on the authoritarian states of Central Asia and the Caucasus today. From both the right and left, critics have thus counseled engagement and commitment, not in the hope of immediate gains but in the expectation that long-term progress might yet be possible.

The problem still exists today, and the debate continues, most recently in the cases of Vietnam, Cuba, Saudi Arabia, Rwanda, Myanmar, and Iran. In all six instances the Obama administration and its predecessors, as well as European countries, have extended opportunities and encouragement to regimes that are generally judged to be anti-democratic, repressive, paranoid and, in the case of Iran, dangerous. Western links with Saudi Arabia remain close, in spite of the fact that men advocating a constitutional monarchy, or women who drive a car or travel without the permission of their male guardian, are severely punished there. Jordan remains a close ally, notwithstanding controls over religious life that are far in excess of what exist in the Central Asian countries that the State Department regularly criticizes. The case of Turkey has already been mentioned, in which the U.S. and EU have been mute in the face of growing authoritarianism. In these and many other cases, the U.S. adopts a double standard for one of two reasons: first, because it believes that in the case of these countries other considerations are more important than democracy and human rights; or, second, it hopes thereby to create an environment that will in the long run foster positive change.

Such an approach is not wrong. But it should be noted that it is justified solely in terms of what might happen in the future, not in terms of present performance as measured by some absolute standard. Such a calculus has rarely, if ever, been brought to bear in the case of countries of Central Asia or the Caucasus. A rare exception was when the State Department in 2016 shelved its objections over developments in Tajikistan because of that country's importance to security in Afghanistan's neighborhood. Critics claim it has done the same with respect to Uzbekistan, but others argue that many of the most damning criticisms of Uzbekistan are based on faulty or incomplete evidence. Otherwise, the U.S. has been quite severe, coming close to cutting ties with Azerbaijan and Turkmenistan during the late Obama years and otherwise throughout both regions "holding their feet to the fire."

Have the "difficult" states of the Caucasus and Central Asia warranted the severity of U.S. policy towards them? Are they all so lacking in promise for the future as to justify the rigorous application of standards that are not systematically applied elsewhere? Has the U.S. failed to consider whether these countries have the potential to evolve in directions it considers favorable? Finally, should America apply its standards so strictly in these countries when it does not do so elsewhere, simply because the countries of the Caucasus and Central Asia are small and weak?

A common feature of American policy throughout the Caucasus and Central Asia is the failure to connect local issues with the broader international context of which they are inseparably a part. Thus, the Karabakh issue is not just a local conflict arising from ancient enmities, as U.S. policy has wrongly assumed, but a key element in Russia's effort to build and sustain a dominant voice in post-colonial countries it once ruled. Similarly, Uzbekistan and Turkmenistan have not adopted isolationist stances because they are ruled by congenital autocrats who fear influences from abroad. Rather, they do so because they face existential security threats that their western partners fail to appreciate. They view isolationism as the best tool available to them. Time and time again the State Department has underestimated the degree to which the problematic initiatives by governments in the Caucasus and Central Asia are their best response to manipulations by neighboring great powers.

One can find fault with America's forbearing approach to Vietnam, Cuba, Saudi Arabia, Rwanda, Myanmar, and Iran. But if it is applied to these countries, several of which pose far more serious down-side risks to American interests, why should it not be applied equally to the "difficult" states of Central Asia and the Caucasus? None of them are ruled by Communist regimes, as are Vietnam and Cuba, none is a brutal theocracy as is Iran. Quite the contrary, all have made substantial progress in areas pertinent to western values and interests and, for all their problems and difficulties, all have real and enormous potential to serve as models of secular and modern states in a region dominated by various forms of obscurantism and retrogression.

Both the U.S. and Europe must apply to Central Asia and the Caucasus the same kind of thinking which, for better or worse, has shaped recent approaches to Vietnam, Cuba, and Iran, and significantly expand the up-side horizon of its engagement. At a time when Cuba and Iran have persisted in old and negative types of behavior, and when the Vietnamese Communist Party has walled itself off from positive change, countries of the Caucasus and Central Asia are undergoing dynamic and peaceful evolution, in most cases under certifiably modern leadership. The risks arising from deeper engagement are few, and the potential benefits high.

EMBRACING A REGIONAL APPROACH

One can reasonably argue that neither the Caucasus nor Central Asia constitutes a region in the full geopolitical or economic sense. After all, border conflicts and fights over water and energy exist across Central Asia, while Armenia and Azerbaijan have remained virtually in a state of war since 1992. Nor has regional comity been enhanced by cordial relations among leaders, several of whom long abused one another in public settings.

If this were the whole story, the U.S.'s present focus on bilateralism would makes sense and the recent American and European moves towards a more regional approach could be dismissed as polite concessions to local demands and nothing more. But numerous changes in Central Asia are laying the foundations of a new regionalism there, and important developments in the Caucasus between Georgia and Azerbaijan cannot advance further without a deepened regionalism. This calls for a reassessment of western tactics in both regions and for a fundamental rethinking of the strategy itself. A combination of external and internal developments across the Caucasus and Central Asia necessitates such a change.

The external factors pertain, first, to sovereignty and security, the overriding concern of governments in both regions. These arise both from geopolitical and economic changes since about 2005. Of the former, the chief source of change has been the rise of Vladimir Putin's Collective Security Treaty Organization (CSTO), his Eurasian Economic Union

(EEU), and the unstated but barely disguised political agenda that goes with them. Kazakhstan's President Nazarbayev has declared many times that his country would quit the EEU if it ventured into the political sphere. Nonetheless, this has already happened in both overt and covert ways. Barely had the ink dried on Kazakhstan's accession agreement than Putin broached his idea of a currency union, which Kazakhstan immediately rejected as political. Putin and his deputies have followed up with other such probes. With little choice in the matter, Kyrgyzstan and Armenia have already joined Kazakhstan as EEU members. It remains to be seen whether Kazakhs and other members will succeed in confining the EEU to business and economic affairs, and whether, and for how long, other countries will resist joining. Meanwhile, Uzbekistan found the developments so threatening that it left the CSTO in 2013. Following the death of Islam Karimov, Uzbekistan's new acting president Shavkat Mirzioyev in September 2016 used his first public statement to declare that his country would join no military or security alliances.

Central Asian countries have, without exception, welcomed Chinese projects and investments, especially in the fields of transport and energy. Seeing them as a useful counterweight to Russia, they effectively elicited Chinese backing when, at an SCO summit in Dushanbe in September 2008, they refused to approve Putin's 2008 invasion of Georgia. Similarly, Uzbekistan worked with Beijing to roll back Putin's effort in 2010 to establish a Russian base in the Ferghana Valley. No region stands to benefit more from China's New Silk Road initiative than Central Asia, with the Caucasus a close second. At the same time the sheer weight of China's presence poses potential threats that are widely recognized, including loss of economic independence and of demographic identity.

In facing these pressures, states of Central Asia and the Caucasus have to choose between aligning themselves closely with one or another external power, or balancing them all against each other in a positive relationship. Armenia, Georgia, and Kyrgyzstan have taken the first course. All the others seek to balance their positive relations with the main external powers and, by delicately playing them off against each other, preserve as much room to maneuver as possible. If western passivity causes them to lose faith in the balancing process, their fallback position will be to follow Turkmenistan into neutrality and self-isolation. Time will tell whether either of these strategies will work, but two things are clear. First, that strategies based on balance will work only if the West acknowledges and embraces its role in the balances and, second, if regional governments do not allow external powers to play them off against each other.

Having already considered the issue of balance above, let us assert and stress that the only way to discourage other powers from pursuing "divide and conquer" policies in Central Asia and the Caucasus is to build and strengthen links among the regional states themselves. Only a strong *regional* approach to the Caucasus and to Central Asia by the U.S. and EU can achieve this.

Separate from these matters, economic development within both regions demands that the West adopt a comprehensive and deliberate *regional* approach. No country has a big enough domestic market to justify certain major investments, but the absence of good land and air transport between the countries and of open economic relations among them (i.e., tariffs, duties, etc.) prevents most region-wide western investments and projects. All countries recognize this, but most hesitate to initiate the kind of actions that are necessary to achieve these ends. By using their convening power, the U.S. and EU can remove impediments to joint action and foster region-wide initiatives.

Well and good, one might object, but what about the bad blood that exists between many states in both regions? This is undeniably a problem, especially with respect to Armenia and Azerbaijan, but many in both the West and Russia habitually overstate its depth and seriousness. Turkmen tribes and Uzbeks had been fighting since the sixteenth century. But when it became necessary to cooperate in order to open the pipeline between Turkmenistan and China, the two countries quickly put aside their enmity and built what is now the most cordial relationship in Central Asia. Messrs. Nazarbayev and Karimov had often exchanged barbs over the years but trade between their countries has greatly expanded recently, and Uzbek exports to Kazakhstan have passed shipments to Russia and Turkey. And in spite of highly public disputes over Tajikistan's Rogun dam project and other issues, the presidents of Tajikistan and Uzbekistan have begun regularly meeting on the sidelines of international conferences.

Beginning with the BTC pipeline project in the 1990s, economic realities have also made Georgia and Azerbaijan partners. The expansion of east-west and west-east transport in goods across both countries is turning them into a kind of "Land Suez" linking Europe to both China and India. To this extent, regionalism already thrives today in the Caucasus, although the Karabakh conflict prevents its full realization. One must also speak increasingly of a new regionalism that links the eastern and western shores of the Caspian Sea. With new ports in Kazakhstan, Turkmenistan and Azerbaijan, and rapidly increasing transport of goods and energy across that body of water, this broader regionalism must be taken seriously. China, India, Europe and the U.S. all have an interest in its success. But Russia has been militarizing the Caspian and even used it as a base for rocket attacks on Syria. To now, there is no forum where such issues are regularly considered.[17] The EU and U.S., acting alone or in consort with other powers, should provide one, lest what should be an international water corridor become a Russian lake.

To their credit, both the EU and more recently, the U.S. have begun building structures for interaction with the countries of Central Asia and the Caucasus that are regional in character. However, these have yet to be linked with long-term strategies towards either the Caucasus or Central Asia, let alone the region as a whole. Lacking that, the West's regional approach remains bureaucratic and inert. This can be corrected only through much more serious strategic planning in both Washington and Brussels, and by the direct engagement of high-level officials from North America and Europe in the application of the resulting strategies.

FIGHTING IMPATIENCE

With deep respect and admiration, the present authors acknowledge the many and diverse positive achievements in Central Asia and the Caucasus that have been brought about through western collaboration and assistance. No other global power comes close to equaling the U.S. or EU in the range, depth, and sheer scale of their commitments. Yet this does not signify that all is well. On the contrary, it has been necessary to detail both structural and strategic shortcomings, the sum of which is to reduce the effectiveness of western assistance overall, weaken the ability of the regional states to develop and prosper in security, and diminish the West's relationship to these emerging regions. All of these shortcomings can and must be addressed. It is hoped that the suggestions advanced here will contribute to that process, and render the relationships stronger and more beneficial to all sides in the future.

Impatience, especially in the U.S., has inflicted much damage on the West's relations with Central Asia and the Caucasus. It has caused official bodies and non-governmental organizations alike to issue scathing complaints about the lack of progress locally. It has led both Washington and Brussels to make abrupt shifts that they have ended up reversing. The inevitable and invariable result of such ventilating is to harden positions on the other side, diminish cooperation, and slow progress overall. Many unfortunate examples of this process can be cited.

It is true that the need to make annual reports to Congress fosters such impatience in Washington. Analogous problems foreshorten time horizons in Brussels. But this is not really an excuse. Corporate leaders work in an environment where even quarterly reports are demanded. Yet only some of them trim their strategies to accommodate the quarterly reporting. The effective ones maintain a long-term perspective even as they shuffle quarterly reports, and manage to explain and defend it before their shareholders. Such an approach is urgently needed in the case of western policy in Central Asia and the Caucasus. It will replace seemingly random "projectitis" with more focused collaborations, and impatience with tenacity.

ENDNOTES

1. Charles Clover, "Russia Announces 'Spheres of Interests'", *Financial Times*, August 31, 2008. (https://www.ft.com/content/e9469744-7784-11dd-be24-0000779fd18c)

2. Bruce Fein, "Stop U.S. Democracy Promotion Abroad", *Washington Times*, December 24, 2014; Robert D. Kaplan, "Was Democracy Just a Moment?", *Atlantic Monthly*, December 1997, pp. 55-80; Stephen Walt, "Why is America so Bad at Promoting Democracy in Other Countries?" *Foreign Policy*, April 25, 2016. (http://foreignpolicy.com/2016/04/25/why-is-america-so-bad-at-promoting-democracy-in-other-countries/)

3. Stephen D. Krasner, "Autocracies Failed And Unfailed: Limited Strategies For State Building," Atlantic Council Strategy Paper, no. 3, 2016. (http://www.atlanticcouncil.org/images/publications/Failed_States_SP_0315_web.pdf); Merilee S. Grindle has argued this in a number of works, including *Audacious Reforms: Institutional Invention and Democracy in Latin America*, Baltimore: Johns Hopkins University Press, 2000.

4. *Ibid.*, and Krasner, "Autocracies Failed And Unfailed", p. iii.

5. Krasner, "Autocracies Failed And Unfailed", p. v.

6. Nelson Kasfir, "The Conventional Notion of Civil Society: A Critique", *Commonwealth and Comparative Politics*, vol. 36 no. 2, 1998, pp. 1-20.

7. Ana Dinerstein, "The Snail and the Good Government: A Critique of 'Civil Society' by the Zapatista Movement, Mexico", Working paper, London School of Economics, 2009. (http://www.lse.ac.uk/internationalDevelopment/research/NGPA/publications/WP36_Mexico_Dinerstein_final.pdf)

8. Claire Mercer, "NGOs, Civil Society and Democratization: a Critical Review of the Literature," *Progress in Development Studies*, vol. 2 no. 1, January, 2002, pp. 5-22.

9. The paradigm is expressed most clearly in Ahmed Rashid "The Fires of Faith in Central Asia." *World Policy Journal*, Vol. 18, No. 1, 2001; Rashid, *Jihad: The Rise of Militant Islam in Central Asia*, Yale University Press, 2002; Eric Mcglinchey, "The Making of Militants: The State and Islam in Central Asia," *Comparative Studies of South Asia, Africa and the Middle East*, Vol. 25, No. 3, 2005; McGlinchey, "Autocrats, Islamists and the Rise of Radicalism in Central Asia", *Current History*, October 2005; International Crisis Group, *Radical Islam in Central Asia: Responding to Hizb-ut-Tahrir*, Asia Report no. 58, June 2003; *Syria Calling*, Europe & Central Asia Briefing, no. 72, January 2015.

10. Matthew Francis, "What Causes Radicalisation? Main Lines of Consensus in Recent Research", January 24, 2012. (http://www.radicalisationresearch.org/guides/francis-2012-causes-2/)

11. Mohammed Hafez, *Why Muslims Rebel: Repression and Resistance in the Islamic World*, Boulder: Lynne Rienner, 2003, p. 206.

12. Even after the "Arab spring" and the collapse of state institutions contributed to a rapid radicalization of Tunisia's Salafi groups, including growing numbers of terrorist acts, a prominent 2015 study argued that the ruling "moderate Islamist" En-Nahda party did not strike a healthy balance between politics and religion, as it was too focused on constitution-build-

ing. These scholars recommend that the solution of the problem lies in strengthening the political inclusion of the Salafi movement; and that the state "should allow all nonviolent religious actors a voice while encouraging official Imams to compete with Salafi preachers to create a diverse marketplace for ideas." Georges Fahmi and Hamza Meddeb, "Market for Jihad: Radicalization in Tunisia", Carnegie Middle East Center Brief, October 2015. (http://carnegieendowment.org/files/CMEC_55_FahmiMeddeb_Tunisia_final_oct.pdf)

13. Vali Nasr, "The Rise of 'Muslim Democracy'", *Journal of Democracy*, vol. 16 no. 2, 2005, 13-27.
14. Joe Davidson, "Report Blasts Foreign Broadcasting Board as 'Dysfunctional' and 'Ineffectual'," *Washington Post*, 22 January 2013, https://www.washingtonpost.com/national/report-blasts-foreign-broadcasting-board-as-dysfunctional-and-ineffectual/2013/01/22/1f-3b1a84-64cd-11e2-9e1b-07db1d2ccd5b_story.html
15. Broadcasting Board of Governors, https://www.afsa.org/broadcasting-board-governors
16. Tom Kahn, "Beyond the Double Standard: A Social Democratic View of the Authoritarianism Versus Totalitarianism Debate," *New America*, July 1985, reprinted in *Dissent*, Spring 2008. (https://www.dissentmagazine.org/wp-content/files_mf/1389820828d12Kahn.pdf)
17. Nearly all published analyses focus on the upside potential of trans-Caspian transport, not threats to it. Stanislav Pritchin: "Transport Potential of the Caspian Sea: Prospects and Limitations," *Caucasus International*, Vol. 6, no.1, 2016, pp. 1171-26.

The Way Ahead

The preceding chapters laid out the problems in American and European policies toward Central Asia and the Caucasus, and ways to ameliorate them. The preceding chapters identified ten key conclusions in the conceptual and strategic realm, and five in the structural and organizational. Let us here reiterate the concrete conclusions that this book advances for a more fruitful approach going forward. In the former category, the key points are the following:

The Primacy of Sovereignty and Security

Western governments should devote serious attention to the sovereignty and security of the countries of the Caucasus and Central Asia as the necessary and inescapable foundation of long-term and many-sided relationships in both regions, and to this end play a more deliberate and active role as part of the "balances" that define the strategies of many, but not all, regional states.

Consider Assistance an Investment, not a Reward

Western assistance should not be seen as a reward for approaching the finish line in a "race to democracy" but as an investment in countries that are important to a range of American or European interests. Concerning voting and citizen participation, the West should recognize that free and fair elections of national leaders are more likely to be the culmination of a democratization process rather than its starting point.

Promote Good Governance

The U.S. and EU must henceforth treat good governance in all areas affecting citizens' lives as a goal in its own right and as a necessary precondition for democracy, and work with local partners to devise programs that advance this end.

Work With Governments, Not On Them

The U.S., EU, and other donor countries in Europe, must reject the widespread current practice of working *on* the governments of Central Asia and the Caucasus to bring about reforms and change, and instead seek to work *with* them to advance these ends.

Reduce Reliance on NGOs.

Without abandoning support for worthy non-governmental organizations, the U.S. and EU should reduce their one-sided reliance on NGOs and re-examine the false romanticism of "civil society," and specifically the conceit that the development of modern societies and polities can be promoted without enabling institutions.

Support Secular Laws, Government, and Learning

The U.S. and EU should acknowledge that among their core interests in both the Caucasus and Central Asia is in the development and maintenance of states that are free from religious control, secular in their laws and courts, and with educational systems that are open to modern knowledge.

Improve Access to News and Information

The U.S. and Europe must acknowledge that access to global news and information is a basic right not only of cosmopolitan elites in Central Asia and the Caucasus but of the publics at large. The West should embrace the advancement of this right as one of its core strategies and objectives, through a variety of initiatives involving television, the internet and print media, as well as radio.

Use One Yardstick for All

As new states trying simultaneously to transform their political systems and economies while preserving their sovereignty and security, the eight countries of the Caucasus and Central Asia have fallen short in many areas. Yet in evaluating their progress and problems, the U.S. and EU have often applied what amounts to a double standard, making demands on these countries that they have not sought to impose on countries in Asia and Africa. Both the U.S. and Europe must apply to Central Asia and the Caucasus the same kind of thinking which, for better or worse, has shaped recent approaches to countries such as Vietnam, Cuba, and Iran.

Embrace A Regional Approach

The U.S. and EU, while maintaining their strong web of bilateral relations in both the Caucasus and Central Asia, should increasingly focus on regionalism as an emerging and necessary structure for the advancement of Western interests there.

Fight Impatience

The greatest enemy of American and European strategy in the Caucasus and Central Asia is impatience. Western programs need to adopt a more realistic time horizon for their end goals.

These conceptual and strategic principles that should serve as general guidelines for policy in turn lead to the following concrete, structural implications:

Coordinate the 'Three Baskets'

A senior U.S. official should be assigned to accept responsibility for the interagency process and thereby bring about coordination between the issue areas of security and strategic relations, economic ties, and good governance and human rights – and lead an active process involving the various agencies of the U.S. government tasked with relations with the region. In Europe, such functions that exist at the European External Action Service should be strengthened.

Minimize Bureaucratic Stove-Piping within the Regions and Between Them

U.S. and European officials should institute mechanisms to restore coordination of their policies toward the South Caucasus, on one hand, and Central Asia on the other, to remedy the artificial dividing line created in their bureaucracies that effectively make the Caspian Sea a barrier rather than a bridge. Further, a greater degree of coordination between Brussels and Washington is desirable and would be a logical result of the strengthening of coordinating function in each capital. And finally, U.S. and EU embassies in the region can coordinate approaches to a much greater degree than is the case today.

Pursue Comprehensive Negotiations to Identify Synergies

On the basis of greater coordination between the issue areas, or "baskets", of Western interests in Central Asia and the Caucasus, it will also be possible to move beyond unilateral mandates in each field toward high-level negotiations with the regional countries spanning all areas of Western interests. This will open neglected possibilities in the area of trade-offs and *quid pro quos* involving Western involvement in security affairs, economic relations, as well as political reforms and human rights. Western officials will then be able to carry out their task in a manner that advances their interests *in all three spheres together*, and not simply in those areas managed by individual agencies. Rather than frame the discussion as a choice between security, economic reform, and democracy and human rights, Western leaders should approach relations as a negotiation involving delicate and evolving balances between them.

Move Beyond "Naming and Shaming"

This study finds the public hectoring that Western officials often engage in one of the most damaging, and counter-productive, elements of U.S. and European policy toward Central Asia and the Caucasus. As Western policies are coordinated better and comprehensive negotiations with regional states are undertaken, it will be necessary to calibrate the public language of Western leaders to a more constructive and collegial approach to these partner states.

Strengthen Governments' In-House Analytical Capacity.

Finally, undergirding all the proposed steps indicated above, Western governments must end their reliance on uncorroborated information from third party sources, and strengthen their internal analytical capability to understand developments in Central Asia and the Caucasus; and the reports published by Western officials must be accompanied by credible evidence and sourcing.

CONCLUSIONS

To conclude, even healthy people need periodic medical checkups. A careful examination can disclose small problems which might, if unchecked, develop into bigger problems. It can identify habits that over time can negatively affect the person's health, and come up with ways to change them. It can even lead to life changes that can enable the person to achieve his or her goals more effectively while becoming a more valued partner, friend, or neighbor.

This is the spirit in which the authors undertook this study. Far from being a product of handwringing and despair, it arose from a keen appreciation of all that the West has achieved in and for Central Asia and the Caucasus over the past quarter century and a spirit of respect for, and gratitude to, those in government, business, and the voluntary sector who made this possible.

Our aim in reviewing western policies towards these regions is not to hand out posies for good works in the past or to administer scoldings to those whom we found wanting. Far from pretending to issue a report card, our sole reason for carrying out this review of the past has been to identify areas in which practical improvements might be effected in the future and to present those findings in some kind of systematic order.

For all the West has achieved in the Caucasus and Central Asia to date, it has yet to reap the full benefits that a more active and carefully directed relationship with these regions can offer. Conversely, the eight countries in question have had great expectations for their relations with America and Europe but they have yet to garner more than a fraction of these in practice.

A major conclusion of this study is that the legitimate aspirations of both parties in this relationship – Central Asia/Caucasus and US/EU – are fully congruent and fully attainable. Indeed, several fields where the West has barely touched the surface – issues such as good governance, the development of secular laws, courts, and schools, and defense-based security — can bring great benefits to both parties in the relationship, as can the untapped economic interests in trade and transport, among other.

Those who are inclined to find conspiracies lurking in even the most innocuous proposals may leap up at this point and claim that the many suggestions advanced in this report add up to a devious but frontal attack on some other country's supposed "interests" in the region. Such claims arise most persistently from Moscow. To deny them here- even before they have been lodged—would be equivalent to trying to respond to the question, "Are you still beating your wife?" Instead let all readers judge for themselves whether our proposals are in any way directed against the *legitimate* interests of any other country. Bluntly, they're not.

Inevitably, there will be many in the United States and the diverse countries of Europe who will acknowledge the potential benefits to their own countries and to all the countries of Central Asia and the Caucasus of a more active relationship but who will then step back, citing the price tag. This, too, is a red herring. Much that has been proposed here can be exercised by directing existing expenditures into more productive channels.

To be sure, this calls for far more rigorous reviews of existing programs than have heretofore been conducted, and more vigilant attention to their implementation, with an eye to cutting back duplication and sheer waste. Above all, it calls for much more constant and thoroughgoing *coordination* within offices, and among programs, agencies, and governments.

In other words, the key variable in the success or failure of all that has been proposed here is not money but *leadership*. We have set forth numerous areas where such leadership has been lacking, beginning with the definition of each side's interests. We consider it absolutely essential for a single official (in the U.S. the Secretary of State or a close subordinate) to be responsible for negotiating with regional governments a single and integrated package of activities based on trade-offs that in the end brings payoffs to both partners. The absence of this kind of comprehensive negotiation is a principal weakness of western strategy to date and one that can be most easily rectified.

This is not the first time in history that the U.S. and its European friends and partners have been called on to render help and assistance to emerging countries. They have been doing so for three-quarters of a century, and with results that strengthen western security and economic life in ways that western tax-payers can be proud. To be sure, there have been mistakes a-plenty. But even as we acknowledge these, let us also note the capacity of western countries to acknowledge and learn from their mistakes, and then introduce mid-course corrections that enable them to proceed in a strategic manner.

Political and economic development is not a sprint but a distance run, in which clarity about ends and means, leadership and, above all, *tenacity* are the key determinants of success. If the West, in this long game, can now muster these qualities and apply them to its relations with the countries of the Caucasus and Central Asia, it will prevail. And all parties to the relationship will benefit far more even than during the past quarter century.

AUTHORS

S. FREDERICK STARR is Chairman of the Central Asia-Caucasus Institute & Silk Road Studies Program, a Joint Center whose components are affiliated, respectively, with the American Foreign Policy Council in Washington D.C. and the Institute for Security and Development Policy in Stockholm. The Founding Chairman of the Central Asia-Caucasus Institute, Starr is a Distinguished Fellow at the American Foreign Policy Council. His research focuses on issues of social and economic development in Central Asia, particularly the salience of continental transport and trade. Starr was educated at Yale, Cambridge and Princeton. He was founding director of the Kennan Institute and is a former President of Oberlin College and the Aspen Institute. He contributed to the establishment of the University of Central Asia, of the Nazarbayev University, and of the ADA University in Baku. He is the author or editor of some twenty-two books and 180 articles, and the recipient of five honorary degrees.

SVANTE E. CORNELL is Director of the Central Asia-Caucasus Institute & Silk Road Studies Program Joint Center. Cornell was educated at the Middle East Technical University and Uppsala University. He is a co-founder of the Institute for Security and Development in Stockholm, Sweden, and a Senior Fellow at the American Foreign Policy Council. He previously taught political science and Eurasian affairs at the University of Uppsala and at Johns Hopkins University-SAIS. He focuses on national security, regional politics, and conflict management issues in the Caucasus, as well as in Turkey, Southwest and Central Asia. He is the author or editor of eight books and some 100 articles.

Index

9/11, 10, 40, 46, 48, 59, 60, 62, 63
Abkhazia, 18, 49, 62
ADA University, 26, 54
Afghanistan, 6-7, 9, 11, 31, 36, 42-43, 45, 48, 50, 53, 59, 63-64, 83, 85, 92, 95, 96, 101, 112, 132, 138, 143
Afghan War of 1979, 40
Africa, 8, 21, 31, 45, 153
Akayev, Askar, 25, 82
Aliyev, Ilham, 51-52
Al-Qaeda, 11, 43
American Chamber of Commerce, 66
American University of Central Asia, 54
Andijan Crisis, 57, 95
Annexation of Crimea, 46
Aral Sea, 60
Armenia, 5-6, 16, 20, 22-27, 30, 45, 50, 57-58, 65, 76-77, 82-86, 96, 129, 144, 145, 146
Armenia-Azerbaijan Conflict, 23, 30, 47, 62, 66, 84, 115
Asia, 8, 12, 22, 31-32, 45, 80, 104
Asia Development Bank, 64-66
Asian Infrastructure Investment Bank, 105
Assassination of Armenian Prime Minister, 48
Astana, Kazakhstan, 23, 81
Australia, 66, 134

Authoritarianism, 29, 33, 36, 43, 78, 81, 99, 128, 142
Ayatollah Khomeini, 92
Azerbaijan, 5, 10, 16, 17, 20, 21, 25-30, 36, 41, 43, 45, 57, 61, 65, 76, 77, 82-84, 86, 88, 93, 96, 101-102, 104, 128, 129, 134-135, 139, 143, 144, 146,147
Azerbaijan-Turkmenistan Pipeline Project, 52
Bahrain, 8
Bakiev, Kurmanbek, 25
Baku, 22
Baku-Tblisi-Ceyhan Pipeline (BTC), 51, 54, 66, 113, 133, 146
Baltic Region, 42, 58, 90, 96
Beirut, 92
Belarus, 7, 50, 75
Bishkek, Kyrgyzstan, 54
Black Sea, 12, 52, 112
BP, 41, 51, 83
Brezhnev, Leonid, 17
British Technical University in Kazakhstan, 54
Broadcasting Board of Governors, 141
Bucharest Summit, 49
Bush Administration, 46-49
Bush Doctrine, 48
Bush, George HW, 12, 47, 75-76, 93
Bush, George W, 12

Canada, 58, 134
Canadian Department of Foreign
  Affairs, 57
CAREC Program, 65-66
CASA-1000 Electricity Project, 53, 64,
  66
Caspian Sea, 7, 10, 12, 42, 50, 51, 53,
  112, 147, 153
Caucasus, 5-21, 23-25, 27, 29-32, 34-
  36, 39-40, 42-47, 49-51, 54-56,
  58-59, 61, 65-67, 77-78, 80-83, 85,
  87, 90, 92, 94, 96, 97-102, 104-105,
  108-109, 111-115, 118, 122-129,
  132-134, 137-148, 151-156
Central Asia, 6-13, 15-21, 23-27, 29-
  32, 34-36, 39-40, 42-51, 53-57, 60-
  67, 78-82, 84-87, 90, 92-99, 101-
  102, 104-105, 108-109, 111-115,
  118, 119, 122-129, 132-135, 137-
  148, 151-156
Central Asia Caucasus Institute, 53
Central Asia Energy and Water Devel-
  opment Program, 64
Central Asia 5+1 Format, 45, 102, 115,
  119
Centre for European Policy Studies,
  63
Central Intelligence Agency, 75, 89
Chabahar, 31
Chechnya, 48
Chevron, 41, 53, 103
China, 9-11, 19, 22, 23, 29, 32, 36, 44,
  52-54, 66, 112-113, 119, 122-124,
  140, 145-147
Chirac, Jacques, 48
Clinton Administration, 46-47
Clinton, Bill, 12, 52
Clinton, Hillary, 53
Collective Security Treaty Organiza-
  tion, 50, 145
Color Revolutions, 43
Command Economy, 19-20
Council for Security and Cooperation
  in Europe, 47
Council of Europe, 55, 78
CPC Pipeline, 52
Cuba, 142, 144, 153
Czechoslovakia, 79-80, 130-131
Deep and Comprehensive Free Trade

Agreement (DCTFA), 61
Decolonization, 45
Democratization, 55, 78-80, 90-91, 93,
  97, 99, 117, 124, 126-127, 135, 139,
  151, 154
Department of Commerce, 47, 52, 97,
  110, 115
Department of Defense, 47, 48, 52,
  94, 96, 110, 115
Department of Energy, 47, 52
Department of State, 50, 52-54, 57,
  84-86, 88, 90-94, 96-97, 99
Department of State Bureau of South
  and Central Asian Affairs, 50, 53, 92,
  112
Department of the Interior, 98
Department of the Treasury, 47, 98
Eastern Partnership, 61
Egypt, 104, 137, 142
Energy, 10, 12, 13, 42, 45, 53
Erasumus Program, 54
Erdogan, Recep Tayip, 87
Estonia, 18
Eurasia, 8, 9, 10, 11, 42
Eurasia Foundation, 57, 58
Eurasia Transportation Corridor, 52
Eurasia Economic Union, 23, 44, 61,
  83, 84, 124, 145
Europe, 8-13, 15, 17, 19, 20, 22, 24,
  29, 32, 36-41, 43-44, 51, 75, 78-80,
  83-84, 87, 90, 91, 102, 104, 109,
  111, 113, 115, 122-123, 125, 127,
  134, 140, 142, 144, 147, 151, 152-
  156
European Bank for Reconstruction
  and Development (EBRD), 64-65,
  100, 103
European Court of Human Rights,
  102
European Endowment for Democracy,
  58
European Union, 8, 40, 41-42, 45, 47,
  49, 50, 54-55, 59, 60-61, 63, 67, 77-
  79, 83, 86-88, 93, 99, 100, 102-103
  105, 109, 111-114, 116-119, 122,
  124, 126-128, 131, 133-134, 146-
  148, 152-153, 155
European Union 2007 Central Asia
  Policy, 43, 79

European Union Eastern Partnership, 50, 129

European Union Central Asia Monitoring Program, 62-63

European Union Neighborhood Policy, 43

ExxonMobil, 41, 53

Ferghana Valley, 23, 31, 145

Financial Crisis of 2008, 44

Finland, 58, 100, 127, 131, 132

Foreign Assistance Act, 81, 82, 93, 116

Former Soviet Space, 23, 35, 42-43, 58-60, 77, 80, 82, 87, 90-91, 95, 97, 99, 103, 112, 131, 134, 139

France, 48, 91, 102

Freedom Agenda, 42-43

Freedom for Emerging Eurasian Democracies and Open Markets Support Act (FSA, HR 282), 40, 41, 54, 55, 75-78, 81-82, 84-86, 88-95, 97-100, 108-109, 117,126-127, 138

French Revolution, 137

Georgia, 5, 8, 16-21, 24-31, 34-35, 42-43, 45, 48-49, 51, 52, 55, 57, 60-61, 65, 80, 82-89, 95-96, 99, 100, 122, 125, 128, 129, 134, 144-146

Georgian-American University, 54

Germany, 11, 54, 58, 100, 105,

Ghani, Ashraf, 132

Gorbachev, Mikhail, 17

Great Britain, 41, 91, 100

Gulyamov, Kadyr, 95

Gwadar, 31-32

Good Enough Governance, 126-128

Helsinki Accords, 87, 97, 118

Helsinki Final Act of 1975, 39, 76-77, 99, 110, 133

Human Rights, 12-13, 42, 45, 77-80, 84-85, 88, 90, 91, 93, 97, 99-100, 110-111, 117-118, 134, 143, 153-154

Hybrid Warfare, 35

Hydrocarbons, 19, 28

Independence, 21, 23, 27, 30, 37, 39-41, 45-46, 48-49, 80, 99

India, 9, 11, 32, 53, 60, 78, 112, 146-147

Indian Ocean, 19, 31

Indonesia, 66

Indus Region, 10

Institutional Reform, 15-17, 24, 34, 51, 78

International Foundation for Electoral Systems, 56-57

International Law, 12

International Monetary Fund, 25

International Republican Institute (IRI), 56, 97

Invasion of Georgia, 2008, 8, 13, 30, 34, 40, 44, 49-50, 62, 96, 145

Iran, 6, 9, 11, 12, 29, 31, 36, 42, 45, 52, 84, 92, 101, 139, 141-142, 144, 153

Iraq, 8, 12, 36, 49-50, 139

ISIS, 36, 87

Islamic Radicalism, 9, 36, 60, 83, 85, 92-93, 101-102, 134-136

Israel, 26

Issue Baskets, 39, 41, 77, 91, 93-94, 97, 99, 109, 114-115, 122, 153

Ivanishvili, Bidzina, 29

Japan, 59, 63, 66, 105, 134

Japan + Central Asia Program, 63

Jordan, 142

Kabul, Afghanistan, 43

Karimov, Islam, 25, 145-146

Karzai, Hamid, 43

Kerry, John, 77, 108

Kazakh Gas Export Pipeline, 28

Kazakhstan, 5, 10, 19, 22-23, 26-30, 41, 48, 52, 54, 57, 59, 63-66, 81, 84, 90-91, 65-96, 102-104, 145-147

Kosovo, 49

Kyrgyz Internal Conflicts 2005-2010, 21, 34

Kyrgyzstan, 5, 17, 19, 21, 23-24, 27-30, 34, 48, 50, 53-55, 58-60, 65, 80-85, 89-92, 99-100, 103-104, 124, 127, 131, 135, 145

Laicite, 25, 101

Latvia, 58, 96

Malaysia, 66

Manas NATO Base, Kyrgyzstan, 81, 83, 92, 95, 124

Market Economy, 25, 41, 77, 126, 134

Medvedev, Dmitry, 123

Middle East, 9, 10, 16, 36, 45, 60, 101, 104, 139

Mirzioyev, Shavkat, 145
Moldova, 51, 61, 86
More for More System, 86,
Muskie Fellowship, 26, 55
Myanmar, 142, 144
Nagorno-Karabakh, 18, 29, 51, 143, 146
Naming and Shaming, 57, 116, 154
National Democratic Institute (NDI), 56, 97
National Security Council, 51-53, 94, 111, 115
NATO, 11, 20, 42-43, 47-49, 62-64, 83, 87, 92, 94-96, 103, 113, 118, 122, 124
Natural Gas, 19, 27-28, 39, 41-42, 50-51
Nazarbayev, Nursultan, 84, 145-146
Nazarbayev University, 26, 30, 54
Netherlands, 41, 58, 100
New Silk Road Initiative, 44, 53, 60, 66
New Silk Road Economic Belt Initiative (China), 54, 65, 145
Niyazov, Saparmurad, 81
Northern Distribution Network, 11, 64, 96,
Obama Administration, 46, 53, 142-143
Obama, Barack, 8, 54, 94
Oil, 9, 11, 19, 25, 27-28, 34, 39, 41-42, 50-51
OSCE, 47, 84, 87, 97-99, 110
Pakistan, 9-12, 31, 53, 60, 83, 135, 139
Parliamentary Republic, 22, 24, 29, 55
Partnership for Peace, 12, 43, 48, 94, 96
Poland, 80, 130-131
Privatization, 16, 25, 33
Putin, Vladimir, 9, 35, 43-44, 83-84, 89, 132, 140, 145
Qatar, 83
Radio Liberty, 89, 141
Rakhmonov, Inomali, 81
Realpolitik, 43
Reset with Moscow, 44
Rice, Condoleezza, 49
Rose Revolution, 2003, 13, 42, 55, 128
RT, 140
Rumsfeld, Donald, 12

Russian Federation, 9-11, 16, 18, 22, 23, 25, 28, 29-32, 35-36, 40, 42, 44, 45-46, 48-53, 62, 66, 75, 79, 89, 96, 104-105, 112-113, 119, 122-124, 132, 140-141, 145-147, 155
Russia-Ukraine Energy War, 113
Rwanda, 142, 144
Saakashvili, Mikheil, 17, 128
Salafism, 26
Saudi Arabia, 87, 142, 144
Sarkozy, Nicolas, 13, 49
Secularism, 9, 12, 25, 27, 36, 104, 133, 137-138, 152, 155
Senate Foreign Relations Committee, 96, 118
Shadow states, 21
Shavardnadze, Eduard, 51
Singapore, 66
South Korea, 66, 105
South Ossetia, 18, 49, 62
Spheres of influence, 49
Sweden, 41, 58, 83, 86, 100
Switzerland, 41, 54, 58, 100
Syria, 8-9, 36, 147
Taiwan, 66, 105
Talbott, Strobe, 47, 50
Tajik Civil War, 81
Tajikistan, 5-6, 17, 19-21, 23-24, 27-29, 48, 53-54, 58-59, 64-65, 81, 90-91, 101, 103-104, 143, 146
Taliban, 11, 43, 60
TAPI Pipeline, 53, 83, 113
Tashkent Technical University, 26
Trans-Afghanistan Pipeline Project, 53
Tokayev, Kassym-Jomart, 22
Turkey, 6, 9, 10, 12, 23, 25, 29, 36, 45, 66, 87, 102, 104, 134-135, 137, 139, 141-142, 146
Turkmenistan Gas Export Pipeline, 28
Turkmenistan, 5, 10, 19, 22-25, 27, 29, 30, 41, 48, 53, 56, 59, 65, 81-84, 95, 103, 135, 143,145-147
Turkmenistan International University, 26
Turkmenistan-China Pipeline, 52
Ukraine, 22, 35 43, 45, 49, 51, 61, 75
United Nations, 48, 131, 142
United States, 8, 22, 29, 35-37, 39-42, 44-45, 47-49, 51-53, 55, 59-60, 62-

63, 66-67, 75, 77-87, 89-92, 97-105, 108, 110-119, 121-126, 131, 133-134, 140, 142-144, 146-148, 151-156
University of Central Asia, 54, 58
University of Georgia in the Caucasus, 54
US-Afghan War, 50
US Coast Guard, 98,
US Information Agency, 88
US Invasion of Iraq, 43, 50, 59
USAID, 41, 43, 55, 57-61, 63-64,67-72, 82, 84-86, 89-91, 93-94, 102-103,126
USSR, 15-18, 28, 30, 32, 34, 39-41, 45-46, 59-60, 75-76, 78-81, 87-89, 95, 110, 125, 128-129, 131, 138-140
Uzbekistan, 5, 19, 22-24, 26-27, 29-30, 43, 48, 50, 54, 56-57, 59, 63-65, 81, 83-85, 90-92, 95-96, 101, 104, 118, 129-130, 135, 139, 143, 145-146
Vietnam, 87, 142, 144, 153
Voice of America, 141
World Bank, 53, 60, 64-65, 100, 103, 105, 132
Xinhua, 140
Yemen, 8, 9